this BARREN ROCK

SYLVIE HAISMAN

this BARREN ROCK

1875 A True Tale
of Shipwreck and Survival
in the Southern Seas

ABC
Books

The ABC 'Wave' device is a trademark of the
Australian Broadcasting Corporation and is used
under licence by HarperCollins*Publishers* Australia.

First published in Australia in 2010
by HarperCollins*Publishers* Australia Pty Limited
ABN 36 009 913 517
www.harpercollins.com.au

HarperCollins*Publishers*
25 Ryde Road, Pymble, Sydney, NSW 2073, Australia
31 View Road, Glenfield, Auckland 0627, New Zealand
A 53, Sector 57, Noida, UP, India
77–85 Fulham Palace Road, London W6 8JB, United Kingdom
2 Bloor Street East, 20th floor, Toronto, Ontario M4W 1A8, Canada
10 East 53rd Street, New York NY 10022, USA

National Library of Australia Cataloguing-in-Publication data:

Haisman, Sylvie.
    This barren rock : a true tale of shipwreck and survival in
    the southern seas / Sylvie Haisman.
    ISBN 978 0 7333 2555 7 (pbk.)
    Bibliography.
    Wordsworth, Charlie.
    Wordsworth, Fanny.
    Strathmore (Ship)
    Shipwreck victims – Crozet Islands.
    Shipwrecks – Crozet Islands.
910.452

Cover design by Darren Holt, HarperCollins Design Studio
Cover images: main image from the *Illustrated London News*, based on a sketch by the
    Strathmore's carpenter, John Pirie; all other images by shutterstock.com
Internal design by Alicia Freile, Tango Media
Map by Lotte Kellaway and Alouis Woodhouse
Author photograph by Sandy Rewi Dales
Typeset in 11/15pt Dante MT Regular by Kirby Jones
Printed and bound in Australia by Griffin Press
70gsm Classic used by HarperCollins*Publishers* is a natural, recyclable product made
from wood grown in sustainable forests. The manufacturing processes conform to the
environmental regulations in the country of origin, Finland.

5 4 3 2 1   10 11 12 13

For my family,
the living and the dead

Contents

Illustrations

this
BARREN
ROCK

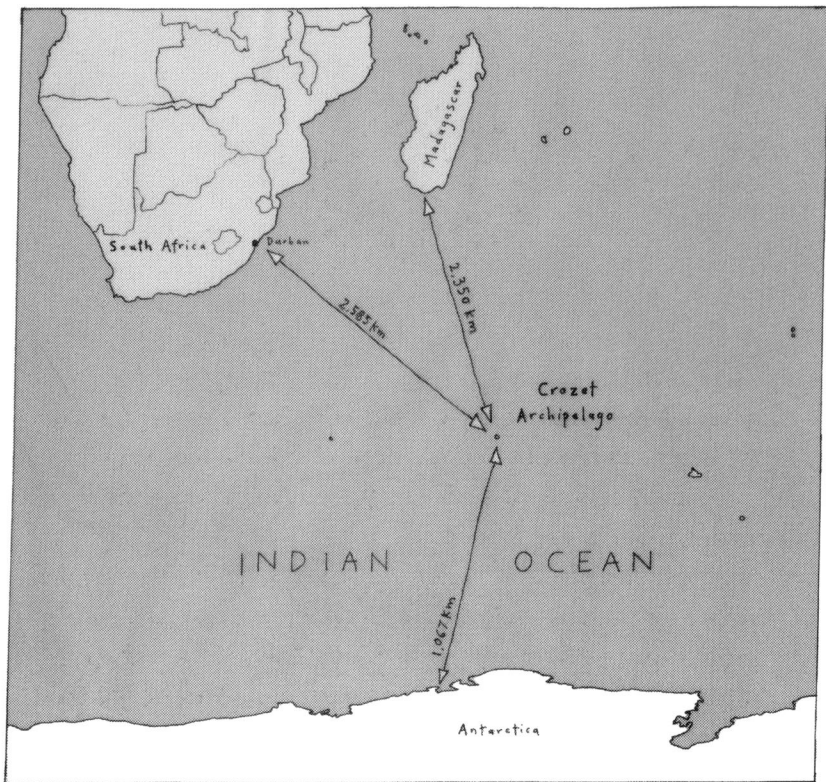

The Crozet Islands, between Antarctica and Madagascar

Imagine one woman, forty-seven men and a three-year-old boy shipwrecked on a tiny sub-Antarctic island. For seven months they eat albatross and burn penguin skins for fuel, before a passing whaler picks them up.

The woman was my great-great-great-grandmother Fanny Wordsworth. She and her son, Charlie, my grandfather's grandfather, were migrating from Scotland to New Zealand when their ship struck a rock in the Roaring Forties, halfway between Antarctica and Madagascar.

I don't remember when I first heard the story. Probably my mother told me when I was still very small, perhaps five or six years old. Maybe we were in the car, driving home to Paekakariki from Hawke's Bay after visiting my grandparents.

'Almost half the people on board drowned in the wreck,' my mother would have said, perhaps looking in the rear-view mirror, flicking the indicator, pulling out to overtake the car in front. 'Mrs Wordsworth only survived because she wouldn't get into a lifeboat with the other women and children — Charlie was far too old to count as a child and she didn't want to leave him.'

'So the little boy on the island wasn't her son?'

'No, he was no relation.'

'How old was Charlie?'

'Twenty-three. He was a grown-up already.'

My mother keeps her eyes on the road.

'The women and children in that lifeboat,' she says, 'they all drowned.'

Or perhaps it was in my grandparents' dining room that I first heard of the shipwreck. In my memory it is a dark room, with light switches and door handles too high to reach. There's a gigantic carved Victorian sideboard laden with flowered china, a silver teapot. We sit around the neatly set table: milk-jug, butter-knife, jam-spoon. At home, milk pours straight from the bottle and the same knife does for butter and jam. But things are different here: you must be polite and tidy; you must speak properly. My grandparents are old, with grey hair and withered, pouchy skin, false teeth and trembling hands. They wear hats

The whale's tooth carved by Charlie Wordsworth and handed down to my grandfather

out of doors, they smell of talcum powder and old-people's clothes, they call me 'dear'.

'Here you are, dear,' says Granddad, holding out a whale's tooth covered in scrimshaw.

He tells me that Charlie did the carving, after the tooth was given to him by a sailor on the whaling ship that rescued the survivors.

'Be careful, dear — it's very old.'

The tooth is yellowy-white, almost as long as my five-year-old forearm. It is carved with a ship in full sail. Under the ship is a picture of an island. Above it are the American flag, the flag of the British Royal Navy, and the month and year of the rescue: 'JAN 1876'.

'The British flag is for the *Strathmore*,' says Granddad. 'The ship that was wrecked. She was from Scotland. And the American flag is for the *Young Phoenix*, the American whaler that rescued them.'

My grandfather was in his sixties when I was a child, which does not seem old to me now. At sixty-five my father wears T-shirts and sneakers, builds garden sheds, surfs the internet. But at sixty-five my grandfather was old — a pipe-smoking, cufflink-wearing, handkerchief-carrying relic from a different time, the far-off 'olden days' when everyone spoke properly and never said what they really thought.

As a child I wanted to visit the olden days. How would it feel to travel by sailing ship, wear strange and complicated clothes, live without plastic and electricity? But I knew I'd have nothing to say to anyone who lived there — the olden days were clearly full of old people. My shipwrecked great-great-great-grandmother and her son would be remote, neatly pressed beings to whom one must be polite.

Then, when I was a teenager, a relative gave my mother a typed transcript of two letters written by my ancestors on board the rescue ship, describing the wreck and their time on the island. The letters were meant for their family back home in Scotland and England, the relatives who'd given them up for dead.

The transcript was typed in capitals, and was over twenty-five pages — but I was enthralled. The voices of my forebears Fanny and Charlie Wordsworth spoke directly to me from the past. Some of the language was a little quaint, but the voices were vivid and real. They made jokes, talked about their sadness and fear, about their dreams, and the relief and joy of rescue. It was as if Granddad told me about a girl he had a crush on in primary school, as if the olden days had burst out of sepia restraint into full colour.

I read the letters, marvelled at them, talked about them, then put them away and forgot them — till about four years ago, when this story of shipwreck began to acquire a new urgency for me. Several things happened around the same time: my mother got cancer, my marriage broke up, a woman who'd been like a mother to me died, and I abandoned a novel I'd spent years working on. In various ways I was confronted with failure, with losing what I wanted most — love, a sense of belonging, success as a writer — and with death.

My ancestors' story spoke to me. They, too, must have wanted something badly — no-one would risk that dangerous voyage without strong motivation. Setting sail for New Zealand, they fetched up on another island on the far side of the world, where they suffered, struggled and believed they would die. The story of their survival was also the story of mine — if Charlie had died, I would not have been born. Of course, I knew the story's ending — my very existence was the proof of Charlie's rescue, at least — but there was so much else I didn't know. What was it they wanted so badly? What were their lives on the island really like? What kept them going when they lost hope? Who were these people, my ancestors, and how had they changed by the time they were rescued?

I became curious, too, about their shipmates — especially those whose voices had been lost, and those who were *not* choosing to change their lives, but were swept along in the current of others' choices. In particular, I found myself drawn to barely literate able seaman Black Jack Warren and three-year-old Wattie Walker. While several of the survivors left detailed accounts of the wreck — including second mate Thomas Peters, third-class passenger Robert Aitkenhead Wilson and fifteen-year-old apprentice Harold Turner, whose voices all appear in these pages — Black Jack and Wattie left no words behind them. Very little information on Black Jack remains, but of all the sailors he was by far the most talked about in the survivors' accounts. A natural leader, he was alternately admired and distrusted, feared and beloved. Wattie Walker was the only child to survive the wreck — though hardly unscathed. Not only unable to read or write when he boarded the ship, Wattie was still learning to speak. What could Wattie's and Black Jack's stories teach me? What could I salvage from the tale of the *Strathmore* survivors to help me find my way in the world?

I

Before

Why does anyone travel, let alone emigrate? At homesick moments in my own life, I have been known to declare that half the trouble in the world could be avoided if people would just stay put. Most wars, all homesickness, many epidemics, much anxiety and sadness, a mountain of lost luggage, a gutful of motion sickness and debt would all disappear, not to mention shipwrecks and other travel-related accidents.

Equally arguably, people as often as not leave home to avoid the other half of the trouble in the world, such as poverty, boredom, political oppression, bad weather, annoying relatives, lack of educational opportunity and so on. People *will* move about. My ancestors were doing it in the 1870s, and I've done it myself on a less dramatic scale.

Even for First World citizens in the twenty-first century, with aeroplanes and international removalists, mobile phones and the internet, the experience of moving countries — no matter how exhilarating and enlightening it can be — tends toward the expensive, the administratively complicated, the emotionally exhausting. If merely moving house ranks high in the list of top ten most stressful life-events today, right up there with bereavement and divorce, how much more daunting was inter-hemisphere relocation in the 1870s?

Consider the matter of cost. In 1875, a London-based craftsman in the building trade could spend two months wages on a one-way steerage passage from London to Otago, whereas in 2009, a skilled trades worker in the UK might pay less than one and a half week's wages for an economy airfare to New Zealand — and that's a return ticket.

Or convenience: a flight from London to New Zealand takes around twenty-four hours, about a hundred times faster than a three- to four-month sailing-ship voyage. Air travellers dreading long delays might be consoled by recalling that nineteenth-century sea voyagers thought themselves fortunate if their ship arrived within two weeks of the scheduled date.

Or comfort. Shipboard living conditions were generally unpleasant. In steerage, the space between floor and ceiling could be less than 1.8 metres, and passengers could expect overcrowding, poor food, dirt, damp bedding, rats, fleas, lice, cockroaches, flooded living quarters and bad smells from latrines and livestock.

While it is true that 21st-century air travellers run the risk of deep vein thrombosis, terrorist attack, full-body searches and plane crashes, these perils are rare and not always fatal. But nineteenth-century migrants to New Zealand were at real risk of dying en route. Shipwreck and fire were a threat on every voyage, and mortality rates were high. Even when ships arrived at their destinations safely, deaths at sea were common. Children were at greatest risk. In the 1870s, twenty per cent of infant passengers under one year of age died during voyages between Britain and New Zealand — one child in every five. On board the *Aldergrove*, a ship that arrived in Port Chalmers, New Zealand, in July 1875, measles killed twenty children. During one 1865 voyage from Britain, fifty-six people — all but two of them children — died before their ship reached Auckland. The causes of shipboard death were various, but diseases such as typhus, typhoid and cholera, related to overcrowding and poor hygiene, were common and often fatal. Possibly one of the least appealing ways to die on board ship was from the complications of seasickness (including dehydration, heart failure and convulsions), although passengers who suffered seasickness for months on end may have envied, at their most desperate moments, those who expired from the complaint.

Quite apart from the differences in cost and convenience, discomfort and danger, the experience of migrating to the other side of the world in the nineteenth century differed profoundly from modern air travel because for most travellers it was almost certainly a one-way experience, parting them forever from the homes, family and friends they left behind. Those migrations were experiences capable of dividing lives in two far more neatly than any 21st-century relocation — there was life *before* and there was life *after*, with very little intermingling between the two.

So why, in the spring of 1875, would a genteel Scotswoman of almost fifty, my great-great-great-grandmother, widowed for twenty years, leave the town of her birth for a new life in the colony of New Zealand?

Fanny Wordsworth, Lady

Fanny Wordsworth had no bad debts to run from. There is nothing to suggest she was looking for a new husband. The late Samuel Wordsworth had left her a comfortable income, and her 'Profession, Occupation, or Calling' — as described on the *Strathmore*'s passenger list — was 'Lady'.

She was not embarking by herself, of course. Her 23-year-old son, Charlie, was to be her companion on the voyage. Migrating to New Zealand was probably his idea. If Fanny let him go without her she'd be all but alone in Edinburgh — her only other living child, 29-year-old Fanny Rosamond, had married an Englishman two years earlier and gone to live in Lancashire.

Fanny was close to both her children. If her only motive for leaving Edinburgh was to be near one of them, she had no need to move to New Zealand. Why didn't she follow her daughter to England instead?

Perhaps Charlie was her favourite. Maybe she disliked Lancashire. Maybe she did not get on with Richard Butcher, Fanny Rosamond's husband. Perhaps all these things were true.

But Fanny was surely not leaving the town she'd lived in all her life because she counted on making a permanent home with

My great-great-great-grandmother Fanny Wordsworth

her son, or even living near him, if the events of later years were anything to go by. At the time of the voyage Charlie was still single, on the lookout for adventure and opportunity. Even if she expected to live with him, Fanny knew she could not rely on it, or on anything — migrating to the other side of the world was inherently risky. And if Charlie chose to marry once they reached New Zealand, she might not be welcomed into the household of his wife. Fanny Wordsworth was setting off for the far side of the world, at least in part, because the idea appealed to her.

It was a massive step to take at the age of forty-nine. What kind of woman was she, this middle-aged widow poised on the brink of a new life, now mostly remembered not for who she was, but for what happened to her?

The one surviving photograph of Fanny was taken in May 1876, about a year after her departure on the *Strathmore*. Elbow propped on a book-stacked sideboard, she looks calm, collected, self-assured — a woman who knows who she is and where she is going. She also seems younger than her fifty-one years, in spirit as well as in looks.

Though her face, neck, hands and hair are revealed, this is mostly a photograph of a dress — a princess polonaise afternoon gown, all silk taffeta, brocade and faille, with rosettes and flounces and a carefully arranged fishtail train curving toward the camera. It was a new dress — an expensive, fashionable, custom-fitted dress, stiff and rustling, and underneath it lay a substantial hidden architecture of whalebone corset, starched petticoats and a 'dress improver' or bustle.

Inside her massive packaging, Fanny looks a little woman, perhaps not much more than 1.5 metres in height. Like her bustle, worn higher than the mode of 1876, her hair was less fashionable than her dress. The plain centre-parting was stylish when she was in her thirties, still raising her children.

The family commonplace book that belonged to Fanny's daughter-in-law

Not long after Fanny's photograph was taken, her future daughter-in-law attempted to capture something of her character in a commonplace book handed down through my family and emblazoned with the grand name of *Confessions: an Album to Record Feelings & Thoughts*.

Inside the book is a kind of nineteenth-century *Cleo* quiz, with headings such as 'Your favourite virtue' and 'Your favourite qualities in Woman' above blank spaces for recording preferences.

According to the album, Fanny's favourite virtue was Patience. Her favourite qualities in Man were Courage and Truth, while in Woman she preferred Pluck. The fault for which she had the most toleration was Hasty Temper. Her favourite heroine was Marie Antoinette, her favourite drink Champagne, and her favourite occupation, Reading a Good Magazine. Her favourite food was strawberries and cream, her favourite poets Byron, Longfellow and Tennyson, her favourite heroes the Duke of Wellington and Louis Napoléon, the French Prince Imperial.

Fanny's idea of misery was being bitten by mosquitoes and sandflies, and her pet aversion was insects of all kinds. Her idea of happiness was 'Living in London with lots of money', somewhere in the vicinity of Hyde Park, and if she were not herself she would have liked to be a queen. Her state of mind, as she filled in the quiz, was Contentment.

Some months before making her *Confessions*, Fanny wrote to her daughter, Fanny Rosamond. The letter was written at sea, four weeks after the rescue of the *Strathmore* survivors.

Dearest Fanny,
I daresay you never expected to see my handwriting again; but
I suppose I must be the veritable bad halfpenny, and of course
have turned up once more.

She went on writing for over twenty-one pages, telling the story of the wreck, the long months on the island, and the survivors' eventual rescue. Though addressed to her daughter, her words were also meant for wider circulation.

I shall not write more than this one letter, so please send it
to my sisters, and all our relations and friends who may be
interested.

In the autumn of 1876, after Fanny returned to Scotland following the rescue, the letter's audience grew suddenly larger. No longer reserved for sisters and friends, it was published in the September edition of *Blackwood's Edinburgh Magazine* as 'Letter from Mrs Wordsworth, the Lady who Survived the Wreck', alongside Charlie's detailed account of life on the island and unrelated stories such as 'Politics and War reviewed from the Alps: A Wanderer's Letter' and 'A Woman-Hater; Part IV'.

In a draft of her letter, written in a notebook on the way back to Britain, Fanny makes it clear that the narrative was intended for publication from the outset: 'Take care of this letter,' she told her daughter, 'as with Charlie's account of our island experiences, we will try to make it into a little story & publish it for the sake of those friends [who helped us].'

Gratitude toward those who'd helped the survivors may not have been Fanny's only motive for seeking publication. In the course of describing her illness and near death on the island, she referred to 'the famous Red Heart Rum', a little of which did her 'incalculable good'. Charlie's account mentions rum too. 'Get Henry White, of London's, Red Heart Rum,' he advises, 'if you want anything good in that line, it is medicinally better than brandy.'

Red Heart Rum advertisements quoted Fanny's and Charlie's letters for years afterward. According to my grandfather, the manufacturers sent Charlie a case of rum every Christmas for the rest of his life. Perhaps they also paid the Wordsworths some kind of fee — a nice addition to their payment from *Blackwood's*.

The draft letter Fanny wrote in her notebook is otherwise almost identical to the *Blackwood's* version, with mostly minor exceptions. But another interesting deletion refers to the able seaman known as Black Jack, one of the *Strathmore* survivors, and was probably altered for fear of making Fanny appear insufficiently ladylike. After editing, the *Blackwood's* text reads simply: 'Black Jack gave me his own stockings.' The notebook letter includes an extra detail: 'Black Jack pulled off my stockings,

A Survivors Story

Bump! bump! bump! that was all,
and the brave ship shook & shivered
like a human being as if she fore-
saw her doom. I hope none of my
readers may ever experience that
awful feeling. To wake in the
dead of night in a small cabin
with that awful sound grating
on your ears and every vibration
of the timbers repeated ten times
in your own body. Oh! the very
recollection of that night brings
back all its horrors & misery —
You must let me tell my story
in my own way. It may not
be a very good way, but I am
not very good at any thing since
my seven months sojourn on that
desert island. So let me begin
at

A page from the notebook in which Fanny first wrote of her adventures

& gave me his own.' Fanny's published account pays warm tribute to Jack's generosity, but in private she could acknowledge his disregard of decorum in favour of practical kindness. The audacity of removing a lady's stockings — some proof of the boldness for which Jack was known — clearly did not lessen Fanny's regard for him.

Fanny drafted her letter to her daughter on the left-hand pages of her notebook. She had begun the book with a different account of her adventures, written on the right-hand leaves. This original narrative was even more clearly intended for publication than the letter to Fanny Rosamond, though apparently it was not accepted by the *Blackwood's* editors. Titled 'A Survivor's Story', the account begins in the most exciting manner:

> *Bump! bump! bump! that was all, and the brave ship shook & shivered like a human being as if she foresaw her doom.*
>
> *I hope none of my readers may ever experience that awful feeling. To wake in the dead of night in a small cabin with that awful sound* <u>grating</u> *on your ears and every vibration of the timbers repeated ten times in your own body. Oh! the very recollection of that night brings back all its horrors & misery.*
>
> *You must let me tell my story in my own way. It may not be a very good way, but I am not very good at anything since my seven months sojourn on that desert island.*

The piece could not have suited *Blackwood's Edinburgh Magazine* better if Fanny had followed the advice of Edgar Allan Poe's 1838 satirical essay 'How to Write a Blackwood Article'.

'Sensations are the great things,' wrote Poe.

> *Should you ever be drowned or hung, be sure and make a note of your sensations—they will be worth to you ten guineas a sheet.*

*The first thing requisite is to get yourself into such a scrape
as no one ever got into before … if you cannot conveniently
tumble out of a balloon, or be swallowed up in an earthquake,
or get stuck fast in a chimney, you will have to be contented with
simply imagining some similar misadventure …*

Despite Poe's tongue-in-cheek claims, *Blackwood's* was known as a respectable, long-established monthly, with a reputation for avoiding what writer and regular contributor Margaret Oliphant called 'anything approaching to grossness or profane feeling', lest the magazine become 'a closed book to many families'. And although Poe insisted that 'it's not so very difficult a matter to compose an article of the genuine Blackwood stamp', in fact there was a great deal of skill required. Fanny pulled it off with style — she was a confident writer with at least a degree of literary ambition.

Her ambition was far from unbridled, however, for she let her son appropriate almost the whole of her unpublished 'Survivor's Story' — over one-third of Charlie's *Blackwood's* article was either paraphrased or taken word for word from his mother's notebook. And no wonder, as whether addressing her daughter or the British public at large, Fanny's voice was lively and often emphatic — just right for a stirring tale of shipwreck and survival. There are frequent exclamation marks. 'Bed indeed!' she cried. And 'Such shoes!'

Fanny's writing also carried the echo of her spoken voice, connecting her directly with her audience. She used 'Charlie noticed to me' instead of 'Charlie said to me', and 'pulled an oar' for 'rowed'. Because of strong currents, their ship could not 'keep its own', and they waited near the mouth of the Irawaddy River because 'the pilot was not come'. Things that surprised her were 'curious' or 'queer'. Things she liked were 'splendid', 'delightful', 'exquisite' or 'charming'. Big things were 'colossal' or 'enormous'. Things she disliked were 'dreadful', and filled her with 'horror' or 'terror'.

Fanny's spoken voice, of course, was that of a Scotswoman — refined, well-to-do, with family connections in England. Her Edinburgh accent was probably not too far removed from upper middle-class English speech, with the Scots influence lengthening particular vowels. The 'poor fellow' in her letter would have sounded more like a 'puir fellow' out loud, her written 'no easy matter' becoming a spoken 'noo easy matter'. She sounded the rhotic Scots 'r' in words where an upper middle-class Englishwoman would drop them: 'Strathmorre', she would say, 'by dint of harrd labourr', 'anxious worrk', 'frightful dangerr'.

In contrast to the published accounts of most other *Strathmore* survivors, Fanny's *Blackwood's* letter included no direct criticism of others. Her praise for the kindness and bravery of the crew extended equally to the second mate — 'the *beau idéal* of an officer' — and the men who were his rivals on the island, like the sailor Black Jack who gave Fanny his stockings and was 'so generous and kind'.

In other letters we see the sharp edge of her tongue. When writing to the Board of Trade to commend the second mate's conduct, Fanny described various unnamed survivors as 'unreasonable', 'selfish', 'lazy', 'dirty and loathsome'. And in a letter to Fanny Rosamond written on board the *Strathmore*, Fanny set down 'the two first-class ladies' as 'worse than common-place, underbred-women'. Her cabin-mate, Miss Henderson, was 'a weak minded pretentious idiot', though after Miss Henderson's death, Fanny referred to her in *Blackwood's* as 'the poor child' who 'always tended me with the greatest kindness and gentle care'.

Though sometimes harshly critical, Fanny was also empathic and curious, interested in everything around her. Her writings record many encounters with people very different from herself, to whom she responded with an open-minded generosity remarkable for a woman of her class and time.

On board one of the ships that took her back to Britain after the wreck, Fanny depicted the sailors as 'a black crew, most of the men colossal and very handsome and strong: they are a merry lot, and their laugh is worth hearing'. She went on to describe her life on board the ship.

> *I have gained a great deal of nautical knowledge; the captain very kindly takes great trouble with me, and then I have long chats with the 'man at the wheel'.*
>
> *Sometimes the 'man' is a boy, or rather child, elf, or sprite, called Jemmie, very small, and knows as much or more than most in the ship except the captain; up to every mischief, very often in disgrace, but neither captain nor anyone else can keep a serious face with him … He is [from] Liverpool, ran off to sea, and I suppose has given his parents more trouble than half-a-dozen usual boys … half Irish and half Spanish; you can imagine the gypsy beauty of the child.*
>
> *A big black called 'Big Jo', when Jemmie teases him, brings his eyes to bear upon him from his height, and says, 'Go 'way, child.'*

After some weeks, the ship anchored near the mouth of the Irawaddy, where Fanny

> *… had the honour of breakfasting with two turbaned Mussulmans …*
>
> *The little stevedore is quite a bright merry Mohammedan, very stout and upright; he puts me in mind of an Italian singer. He took tea with us, and very kindly took down an enormous turban to show me how it was done.*

The look of things was a frequent topic in Fanny's letters, and she had an eye for beauty. A sea-captain's wife was 'a tall, slender woman, like a lily', while the captain himself had 'the rather long face of the American, but ... is very handsome'. And as one might expect from the (mostly) fashionable lady of the photograph, Fanny paid detailed attention to clothing. On the island where she was shipwrecked she wore 'a suit of manly garments ... Trousers, my flannel petticoat, and a "monkey jacket" completed my outfit ...' She was naturally delighted when the wife of a sea-captain gave her 'a very handsome red wrapper, and various other articles, including a waterproof, and lovely shoes and stockings'. On another ship, the captain presented her with 'a curtain (Dolly Varden print) to make a skirt of — a fancy blue shirt for a bodice, and his own white linen coats for jackets'.

Her writing is also full of references to food and cooking.

The living is good; plenty of nice vegetables, delightful bread, and eatables of all kinds, and lots of preserved fruits and jams. If you have any nice homemade, I can tell you they will suffer in comparison ...

It is delightful to think of new milk and eggs, and abundance of delicious fruit, cocoa-nuts in perfection. I am a great believer in sugar now; I think it cured me of sea-sickness ...

I am bringing home quite a valuable book of receipts which the steward has very kindly given me — quite Yankee notions, and very good ones too. I mean to be no end of a cook when I get home.

The great appetite for life in Fanny's post-wreck letters was partly her response to the unexpected good fortune of having survived: 'I trust I shall never forget all Almighty God has done for us — our life and preservation on the island was all a miracle.' But Fanny's zest and inquisitiveness were surely also due to her temperament. She could have responded to a narrow escape from death by collapsing into nervous anxiety, but instead, judging by her letters, she was energised.

If it was Fanny's curiosity and enthusiasm for novelty that led her down the path of migration and ensured her recovery from shipwreck, was there anything in her earlier life that foreshadowed her willingness to embrace such tremendous changes? How had she arrived at the crucial turning point of leaving for New Zealand?

Fanny Wordsworth was born Frances Young, on 20 April 1825, to middle-aged parents: Elizabeth Calder Young, thirty-three, and Robert Young, forty-four, cashier of the Edinburgh General Post Office. The infant Fanny had at least three older siblings: two-year-old Marianne, nine-year-old Elizabeth and eleven-year-old Thomas. When she was two, Charles Alexander was born. Fanny, perhaps, was fond of her little brother, and later named her son for him.

The Young family was part of Edinburgh's powerful middle class. Bankers, capitalists and professionals made up over twenty per cent of the city's population — far more than in other British cities at the time. Professional men like Robert Young drew steady salaries, worked regular hours and looked forward to pension entitlements. The Youngs were not rich — they kept only one servant — but their position was fairly secure.

Fanny grew up in the prosperous New Town, not too far from Waterloo Place where her father worked in the newly built Post Office building. The year she turned four, the New Town was described in Shepherd and Britton's *Modern Athens: Or Edinburgh in the Nineteenth Century*.

Wide streets, laid out at right angles with each other, and
terminated occasionally by spacious and handsome squares,
give an air of beauty, and even of grandeur, to parts of this
newly formed district ... Built on an eminence, about 200 feet
above the level of the sea, and considerably above the Old Town,
it ... commands varied and extensive prospects ... towering
above the low grounds in the vicinity.

The middle-class population of the New Town was about forty
per cent, double that of the city as a whole. The remaining sixty
per cent was made up of those supplying goods and services
to the professional men and their families: domestic servants,
waiters, shop assistants; keepers of hotels, coffee-houses and
gentlemen's clubs; artificial-flower makers, bird and animal
stuffers, bookbinders, tailors and gardeners; manufacturers of
baby carriages, billiard tables, guns and umbrellas. They plied their
trades from grand shops on the main shopping streets, or from
workshops, carts and street stalls in the back lanes and mews.

Some of these workers returned at night to the narrow
closes off the Old Town's High Street, where they lived in tall,
dilapidated tenements, so overcrowded that single rooms could
house up to a dozen people. 'Half-a-dozen of trades will be
carried on by the denizens of one room,' wrote John Heiton
in 1859 in *The Castes of Edinburgh*, 'shebeening, out-of-door
appleselling, match hawking, newspaper selling, prostitution,
thieving, subletting for an hour to vagrant couples not intent
upon singing psalms'.

Old Town residents might go up to the New Town for work,
but the traffic was largely one way. Little Fanny and her brothers
and sisters had few reasons to venture into the Old Town, and in
their own neighbourhood they were screened from the poorer
district by what Heiton described as 'those fine gardens which ...

tend to keep from the too close view of the New Town gentry the poor population of the Old Town'.

When Fanny was ten, her older sister Elizabeth was married. By the time of Marianne's wedding, Fanny was seventeen. Like her sisters, Fanny was married at the age of nineteen. Like her mother, she married an older man — Mr Samuel Wordsworth Esquire.

At thirty-seven, Samuel Wordsworth was nearly twice Fanny's age, a respectable lawyer and businessman. Though better off than Fanny's father, Samuel was only a first-generation gentleman — old Mr Wordsworth had been a horse-dealer, innkeeper and slum-lord, a literate but not especially grammatical man.

A keen rider and huntsman, Samuel Wordsworth was proprietor of Her Majesty's Repository, a superior kind of horse dealership, where a man, as writer James Greenwood put it in

Fanny's husband, Samuel Wordsworth, in his riding gear

1867, could 'buy a horse or carriage with the certainty that he will not be chaffed by stable ruffians or fleeced by the common horse-sale shark'.

After their wedding on 21 November 1844, Fanny and Samuel moved to Colinton, a semi-rural area some six kilometres west of Edinburgh. They are said to have lived at Spylaw House, built by the owner of a snuff mill.

Within eight months of the wedding, Fanny was pregnant. Over the next six years she had five children. Frances Rosamund was the first, Charles Francis the last. The three in between all died in their first year: two boys, both called Samuel, then a girl, named Sarah for her aunt and grandmother.

After each child died, the Wordsworths moved house. From Colinton they shifted to a terrace house in Baxter Place, back in the New Town. Then they went round the corner to Windsor Street. They lived at number six, with three servants: cook, housemaid and a nurserymaid for Fanny Rosamund, aged five, and baby Sarah, who still had three months left to live.

In late 1851 or early 1852, Samuel bought a house in the parish of Liberton, a countrified district about ten kilometres from the centre of Edinburgh. A substantial stone building with high ceilings and a large garden, the Wordsworths' new home was described by the *Liverpool Mercury* in 1856 as the 'Mansion House of Drumbank ... extremely commodious, and ... admirably suited for the country residence of a genteel family'.

The house was painted and papered and new stables were built. Soon after Samuel and Fanny moved in, their son Charlie was born. No doubt they planned to live there for decades to come.

But only three years later, on 24 November 1855, Samuel Wordsworth died. 'Bronchitis combined with disease of heart', said the death certificate.

Spylaw House, where Fanny and
Samuel probably lived after their
marriage in 1844

Fanny was thirty years old. Her daughter, Fanny Rosamund, was nine, her son, Charlie, just three. Her marriage, supposed to be her vocation for life, had lasted eleven years and three days.

The house was sold. 'It is in first-rate repair,' bragged the *Liverpool Mercury*. 'The valued rent is £85. Fen duty nominal. Upset price £1025.'

And Fanny and the children moved again, probably back to another terrace house in the New Town. Her Majesty's Repository was sold too, and the capital invested to make a regular income for the widow and orphans.

Almost certainly it was after her husband's death that Fanny converted to Catholicism. Like most other Scots at the time, she was born into a Protestant family, married a Protestant and christened her children as Protestants. But by 1863, when she sent eleven-year-old Charlie to a Jesuit boarding school, Fanny and her children were Catholics.

Conversion was a brave move in staunchly Protestant nineteenth-century Scotland. Most of the country's Catholics were poor Highlanders or uneducated Irish migrants, and public office had only been open to Catholics since 1829.

There is no evidence that Fanny's husband had any Catholic leanings. Certainly he had every reason not to convert. In nineteenth-century Edinburgh, success in both business and the law relied on connections. Men traded favours and information in coffee-houses and gentlemen's clubs, and deals were brokered through alliances cemented by family and religious ties. Samuel Wordsworth was not so sure of his position that he would happily risk the ostracism of his peers.

Fanny was unlikely to have converted while her husband lived. But as a widow of independent means she could afford to brave unpleasant social consequences. Very likely she sought the comfort of a new faith in the early years after Samuel's death, as she adjusted to widowhood.

Though highly unusual, Catholic conversion was less outlandish for Fanny than for most of her fellow Scots. She was Episcopalian — almost as bad as being Catholic in the eyes of the Presbyterian majority. Episcopalians celebrated saints' days, answered to bishops and worshipped with a High Anglican prayer book and liturgy. Scottish Episcopalians had supported the Catholic Stuarts when they were barred from the British throne. Episcopalians, too, were regarded as particularly vulnerable to influence from the Oxford Movement, a group of deeply religious English intellectuals who emphasised the Catholic roots of the Anglican Church.

One of the Movement's many followers who ended up converting to Catholicism was the English novelist Lady Georgiana Fullerton, author of books such as *Too Strange not to be True* and *Ellen Middleton* (described by a Lord Chancellor as 'rank popery'). Daughter of an earl and granddaughter of a duke, Lady Georgiana was known for her piety and philanthropy. Listed in

Fanny's *Confessions* as one of her 'favourite prose authors', the novelist became a Catholic in 1846, probably about ten years before Fanny, providing an attractively aristocratic model of the devout lady convert.

Fanny may also have been encouraged by the conversion of several Scottish aristocrats in the early 1850s. But the Oxford Movement never really caught on in Scotland, and most New Town ladies and gentlemen had scant sympathy for 'papists'.

If Fanny's departure from the Protestant community loosened her sense of belonging to Edinburgh, then conversion may have been her first step toward migration, helping to undo her ties to the city of her birth and readying her for a new life among new people.

In the meantime, Fanny lived in Edinburgh's New Town and raised her children. She turned thirty-five, and her eight-year-old son left home to be educated. She turned forty-five, and her 24-year-old daughter left home to be married. Her adult son came home again. She visited her adult daughter in England. She went to mass and confession.

The first thirty years of Fanny Wordsworth's life had held little scope for an independent character. Respectable women sought marriage and motherhood, and Fanny had not strayed from the narrow path laid out for her. But when given the chance to go her own way, she did so. She left her faith for Catholicism. She left her home for the other side of the world. These were remarkable and somewhat risky choices for a woman in her position at the time.

By early 1875, when Fanny was preparing to sail for New Zealand, she had been a Catholic for probably close to half her adult life, and a widow for almost twice as long as she'd been a wife. Nearly fifty years old, she was embarking on what would prove to be an extraordinary voyage.

Charlie Wordsworth, Gent

Like many an adventurous young man before him, Fanny's 23-year-old son, Charlie Wordsworth, was setting sail for the colonies. 'Chas Wordsworth' reads his entry in the ship's papers. 'Occupation: Gent'. Charlie was off to make his fortune, accompanied by his widowed mother.

He was fond of his mother, even devoted to her, but he did not lack independence. Charlie was eight when he first left home, packed off to boarding school with his upper middle-class contemporaries.

At first, he was sent to the Scottish Borders, not too far from home in Edinburgh, so he could return for holidays with his mother and sister. But by the age of ten, he was at college in Derbyshire — a considerable distance back then.

My great-great-grandfather Charlie Wordsworth as a young boy

Probably Charlie missed his mother, as most little boys do when far from home. He did well at his studies, however, and soon after finishing his education he travelled just about as far away from Fanny as he could. Charlie's 1875 voyage on the *Strathmore* was not his first colonial excursion — he'd been out to New Zealand before.

I know next to nothing about his initial journey — neither his date of departure or return, the ships he sailed on, nor his reasons for going or for coming back again. All I can be sure of is that on 31 October 1873, at the age of twenty-one, Charlie was in Auckland: he made a will there and sent it home to his mother. He'd been of age for five months and owned property left to him by his father.

What kind of young man would sail halfway round the globe, presumably in search of adventure and opportunity, and then sail back again to fetch his mother?

Surely Charlie had no strong aversion to travel, nor to spending money. And perhaps, although quite equal to shifting for himself, he enjoyed the company of women, preferring travels with a domestic backdrop over solo expeditions. Certainly he lived the rest of his life as if this were so.

There is no-one alive now who remembers Charlie Wordsworth; no-one who can tell me about him. My grandfather never met him, though he was Charlie's grandson — Charlie died before any of his children married. But my great-aunt Cecil remembers Charlie's youngest daughter, Bessie, as a very old lady who referred to Charlie as 'Papa'. When Bessie recalled his death, my great-aunt said, the tears came into her eyes 'as if it was yesterday'. But Bessie was remembering a father, a married man in his forties, not the young man who walked up the *Strathmore*'s gangway with his mother.

Judging from a photograph taken in Edinburgh near the time of the voyage, he was not bad-looking. He wore his wavy hair

Charlie Wordsworth as a young man in Edinburgh

cropped short; his neatly trimmed moustache gave a masculine cast to an otherwise rather fine-featured face, with full lips, expressive eyes and a certain intensity to the gaze. He looks manly, sensitive — just the kind of young man likely to embark on a colonial adventure.

Outside the frame of the photograph, Charlie was of middle height and medium build with a reddish moustache and light brown hair. What did he sound like when he opened that mustachioed mouth? No doubt he spoke like the well-to-do Edinburgh gentleman he was. Probably his accent was not as Scottish as his mother's after his years of English education. And something of his manner of speaking — and his personality — may be gleaned from a letter addressed to his older sister, Fanny Rosamund. He wrote it in great haste on board the *Strathmore*, about a month before the wreck.

Dear Fanny,
There is a ship bearing down on us, evidently wanting
provisions or some thing & is now lowering a boat, so that I
shall get this letter sent off if I get the chance.

He reported conventionally on the weather and his mother's health. Then, more thrillingly, he moved on to dancing naked on the poop during a thunderstorm and punching a drunk in the face. The 'regular Bacchanalian dance & wash' was performed by 'all the young fellows' in what Charlie modestly described as 'very light habiliments indeed'. He was less modest about the punch, 'which laid… [the drunk] in the scuppers'. Being in a hurry, he wrote very briefly. His tone was light and cheery, and mildly ironic in places: 'I had the honour of giving him two smart raps.'

Like his mother, Charlie filled out a page of *Confessions* in the family *Album to Record Feelings & Thoughts*. He made his entry around the same time as Fanny, fairly soon after their return to Scotland following their rescue, at a moment when his mind was 'in its chronic state of wishing for something'.

They are brief, pithy confessions. If not himself, Charlie intimated, with a degree of self-regard, he would rather be his own twin brother. In Man he valued Manliness, in Woman Impudence, and his chief characteristic was Vanity. The fault for which he had most toleration was 'Laughing when you should not'.

In fiction Charlie admired the comic idealist Don Quixote. His favourite real-life hero was John Evans, though he didn't specify which one. Did he mean the early sixteenth-century Welsh pirate? Or the explorer of the Missouri River? The English archaeologist or the Governor of Colorado responsible for the Sand Creek Massacre?

His regard for Sir Walter Scott, at least, is clear — Scott is listed as both Charlie's favourite poet and favourite prose author. But what can we learn about a young man from his liking for this tremendously popular writer? That his mind was delighted by tales of battle and high adventure, his imagination fired by

Scott's romanticised version of the Scottish Highlands? That he was a man of his time, enjoying what his neighbours enjoyed?

Charlie liked to eat 'Anything when hungry'. His favourite occupation was Riding, his idea of happiness was Champagne, and of misery 'A wet day'. He preferred to live 'Not on the Crozets [where he was shipwrecked]' and his pet aversion was a head wind. His favourite virtue was Truth and his motto was 'Be what you seem to be' — either a modified version of Aeschylus's 'for he wishes not to appear but to be the best' or a quote from *Alice's Adventures in Wonderland*.

> '*Oh, I know!*' *exclaimed Alice, who had not attended to this last remark,* '*it's a vegetable. It doesn't look like one, but it is.*'
>
> '*I quite agree with you,*' *said the Duchess;* '*and the moral of that is* — "*Be what you would seem to be*" — *or if you'd like it put more simply* — "*Never imagine yourself not to be otherwise than what it might appear to others that what you were or might have been was not otherwise than what you had been would have appeared to them to be otherwise.*"'

So what did Charlie seem to be? How did he want to appear to others? A joker, a man of action, a straightforward, self-deprecating character, a man who loved 'Crimson' and 'Roses'?

Some months before making his *Confessions*, Charlie wrote a long account of the shipwreck, almost ten thousand words, which was later printed in *Blackwood's Edinburgh Magazine* alongside his mother's letter. In the account, he is a sober character, serious and formal — '*cum grano salis*', he wrote, instead of 'with a grain of salt'. But traces of humour sneak in. The island's penguins 'looked like fat old gentlemen in white waistcoats', and as the survivors ate the offal-stuffed large intestines of seabirds they 'tried to imagine them sausages'.

Though he cribbed over one-third of his article from Fanny's unpublished story, Charlie's tone was more distant than hers. He began his tale with an overview of the wreck, presenting events he did not witness as objective fact. When recounting his own experiences he focused on what happened rather than how he felt, though he did record brief expressions of disgust — 'ugh! it was bad', and of pity — 'poor fellow'. In place of his personal feelings he described the survivors' collective emotions — 'mortification', 'pleasure', 'fear', 'excitement and hope', 'great disappointment', 'delight and astonishment'. But in contrast to his mother he did not dwell on others, devoting significantly more attention to seabirds than to people. His descriptions of the birds are lively and funny, often anthropomorphic. He noticed their nests and plumage, the appearance of their eggs, and was clearly fascinated by their feeding and mating habits.

No doubt the difference in emphasis between the Wordsworths' accounts was due partly to their different experiences. Fanny's hut-bound days yielded few diversions beyond her observations of her fellow survivors and her own inner life, while Charlie was generally busy out of doors, closer to the birds than to the people and with less time for contemplation.

Throughout his narrative, Charlie referred to Fanny as 'my mother' and was quietly chivalrous toward her, occasionally tipping into gentle and sometimes teasing condescension: when in her own published account she referred to a river from which 'no-one ever returned to tell the tale', Charlie added a footnote. 'Not quite correct,' he wrote, before elaborating his version of the story.

If Robinson Crusoe had been wrecked on a sub-Antarctic island with his mother, rather than on a tropical island alone, his narrative would perhaps have resembled Charlie's. The two share the same foresight and self-reliance, the same methodical approach to problem-solving and resolute focus on self-preservation, and Charlie's account echoes Crusoe's scientific attention to detail: 'I have seen in books of natural history that penguins lay only one egg; now our penguins laid three,' he wrote. 'The first was the smallest, and of a light-green colour; the others whiter and larger, especially the last one.'

He felt the same appreciation as Crusoe for the beauty of the natural world: 'The albatross were very majestic and graceful in their movements. We used to see them, when pairing, bending and bowing to each other like courtiers in the olden time dancing a minuet.'

As well, he shared Crusoe's oblivious disregard for his effect on that world: 'I generally killed and skinned about fifty old penguins [each morning] ...'

Unlike Crusoe, however, Charlie never directly mentioned religion, though he briefly waxed poetic about the 'unfortunate few whom it was our sad task to bury on that bleak lonely island', and whose graves 'lie far from all sounds of human toil', where 'no affectionate hand marks the spot with the humble tribute of flowers'.

This somewhat maudlin passage differs sharply from the rest of Charlie's story. Was he dutifully going through the motions of sorrow, saying what he thought he should say? Perhaps his everyday language did not include words for deep emotion, leaving him no choice but to borrow hackneyed phrases.

Fanny's *Blackwood's* letter shows Charlie busying himself on board the rescue ship by 'painting pictures on the sailors' boxes', washing clothes — he was 'a first-rate washer' — and pulling ropes — 'going through great exertion'. He took her to see the anchor dropped, called her on deck to see the 'queer boats, Chinese junks, sampans, and barges', and had 'a hearty laugh' when his bed on board ship was occupied by visiting stevedores.

She spoke highly of his courage and kindness, his modesty and resourcefulness.

He has shown himself a grand fellow, cool and steady in danger, with all his wits about him. Such tender care he took of me too, never making a fuss about what he did!

You would have thought he had been the only one shipwrecked before. All the others were extravagant and wasteful with clothes, string, &c. He got many out of a difficulty by supplying a little of the latter commodity, and at the last he was the only one with a lashing for carrying his birds. He won the respect of all, especially the sailors, with whom he was a great favourite.

She described how he loved to hear 'all the little stories' about his childhood and Fanny's own youth to enliven gloomy hours on the island. It is through Fanny that we glimpse Charlie's vulnerability: 'One day on the island, when food was scarce and hunting hard, he was quite worn out and burst into tears. Poor fellow! I felt that more than anything that happened to me.'

A tender fellow who hid his feelings, an enterprising and adventurous mother's boy, an educated gent who enjoyed a joke and was a favourite with the sailors — where did he come from, this Charlie Wordsworth?

Charles Francis Wordsworth was born at Drumbank House, on 7 June 1852. His mother, Fanny, was twenty-seven, his father, Samuel, forty-five, and his sister, Fanny Rosamond, six years old. When his father died, Charlie was three.

Did the adult Charlie retain any memory of Samuel? Could he recall the weeks when his father lay dying in the big bedroom upstairs? Or the upheaval of moving into Edinburgh when Drumbank House was sold a few months later? Very likely he remembered the mourning clothes worn after Samuel's death. Months and years of rustling black crepe — a silk cloth that reflects no light and tends to run in the rain. Probably his mother was still in the muted greys and lavenders of half-mourning when Charlie was six years old.

In some way, the little boy absorbed her sadness. Maybe he grew protective of her, as the sons of solo mothers often do.

By the age of eight, Charlie was eighty kilometres from his mother, down in Jedburgh — a town on the Jed Water, just sixteen kilometres from the English border. She'd enrolled him in the Nest Academy, a Protestant preparatory school. If, as I believe to be the case, Fanny Wordsworth and her children converted to Catholicism soon after Samuel's death, it might seem surprising that Charlie was sent to a Protestant school. No doubt his mother would have chosen a Catholic establishment if she'd found one that suited. But most Catholic schools catered for the children of the poor — there were not too many choices for genteel Catholic Scotsmen under the age of ten.

According to the *Glasgow Herald*, the Nest Academy was 'delightfully and healthfully situated' within the close of the ruined twelfth-century Jedburgh Abbey. Both pupils and staff lived in an eighteenth-century house containing, 'on the Ground Flat, a large Private Class Room, 25 by 16, Kitchen, Back Kitchen, Laundry, Milk House, and other conveniences; on the Second and Third Floors, Dining-Room, Drawing-Room, and Nine Bed-Rooms, besides Attic Rooms, Water-Closets, &c., &c.' There were separate schoolrooms, 'with every attention to convenience and comfort. There is ample Play-Ground, and a Garden, Gig-House, Stable, and other Offices; and the whole Premises are walled in, fully supplied with excellent Spring Water, and in every way fitted for the purpose ...'

On census night 1861, the Nest housed twenty-five scholars,

aged eight to fifteen, plus four masters, two matrons and two servants. Charlie shared a room that night with the three other pupils his age.

Boys came from as far away as London and even Australia to attend the Nest. Mostly they were the sons of professionals — lawyers, doctors, clergymen — who went on to become professional men themselves. One of Charlie's contemporaries was the local minister's son, David George Ritchie, later an Oxford-educated philosopher.

Edinburgh's *Caledonian Mercury* advertised the Nest Academy as 'a superior Establishment for the Board and Education of Young Gentlemen', where the 'Course of Study includes Classics, Mathematics, and the various Branches of a Sound and Liberal Education'. The fees were £30 a year for boys under twelve (£5 extra for older boys) with German and Drawing an extra two guineas each. Probably Charlie, who became a skilled amateur draughtsman and landscape painter, took the extra tuition in 'Ornamental Writing, Pencil-Drawing, and Map-Drawing'. Emphasis was placed on Classics, with pupils spending much of their time learning Ancient Greek and Latin. They were also taught French, and 'very carefully instructed in English Reading and Grammar, as well as in the other Branches, including Geography, Arithmetic, Mensuration, and Mathematics'.

Charlie may well have developed his interest in natural history at the Nest, where prizes were given for such items as the Best Collection of Leaves, illustrating their formation; the Best Collection of Insects within two miles of Jedburgh; the Best Collection of Land and Fresh Water Shells; and the Best Specimens of Various Kinds of Grain.

Like many young people, at times Charlie probably felt an outsider in one way or another — perhaps too awkward, too cowardly, too clumsy, too stupid, too handsome, too clever, too

Charlie Wordsworth,
schoolboy rambler

ugly to always feel truly at home with his peers. But in addition to any common-or-garden social handicaps he may have experienced, Charlie really was different from most of the other boys at the Nest.

First, he had no father — nothing to boast of in the way of paternal accomplishments or attributes, nothing to complain of in the way of fatherly punishments or lectures, nothing to add when the talk swung round to Papa's latest letter or present of pocket money. Even worse, Charlie was a Catholic — *Catholic dogs stink like frogs and don't eat meat on Fridays.* Whether he was teased or not, the very timetable of the school marked out his difference from the other boys. The Nest Academy, according to the *Glasgow Herald*, paid 'great attention to Moral and Religious Instruction', including 'Scripture Biography, and the Elements of Sacred Truth', classes which did not cover Catholic teachings. Charlie's time in Jedburgh surely taught him that religion was a matter on which different opinions could be held.

By 1863 Charlie was ten, old enough to be accepted at Mount St Mary's College, a Jesuit boarding school in Derbyshire. Along with the other Catholic colleges in Great Britain at the time, Mount St Mary's had some rather mixed press. According to the *Birmingham Daily Post* on 20 January 1860, the colleges were 'mainly intended for the education of the Roman Catholic priesthood, for it is well-known that the lay education in them is made wholly subservient to that of the "church students", and is consequently at a very low ebb as far as secular and classical learning is concerned.'

By 1886, however, Mount St Mary's was characterised more favourably by Mr John Kirkwood Leys, a Catholic convert and barrister-at-law, who described the college as 'a school for the sons of Roman Catholic gentlemen, where they were prepared for the universities, and for the military and Civil Service examinations, and ... would associate with companions of their own rank'.

How did ten-year-old Charlie experience his new school?

Being Catholic was no longer a problem for him at Mount St Mary's. But his Scots accent made him stand out among the English boys. And though he was used to boarding, Mount St Mary's was a far bigger school than the Nest Academy. The dormitories housed over a dozen boys, the beds lined up in rows — quite a change after sharing a room with just three or four others in Jedburgh.

Also, there were no matrons to look after the boys at Mount St Mary's, no-one to remind Charlie of his mother. The college was an all-male world, with corridors and classrooms full of pupils and priests — boys from ten to eighteen or older in school uniform and men in long black robes, swirling and swishing about them as they walked.

A bell rang at noon and again at six pm for the recital of the Angelus. The scholars must have known the words well: *Angelus Domini nuntiavit Mariae* ... They understood them too, for they were taught largely in Latin, learning to read, write and even speak the language. They were also taught Ancient Greek, philosophy, mathematics and the natural sciences as well as the humanities — literature, history and modern languages.

There was a daily mass, and confession once a month. Formal scripture classes took up perhaps two hours a week, but religion permeated all the other subjects.

Sports were important at the school, and the young priests were not above joining in. Two months after Charlie entered Mount St Mary's it was time for the Easter week sports day, held on the college cricket ground. Perhaps he took part in Putting the Weight or Throwing the Cricket Ball, tried High Jump, Pole Jump or Broad Jump, or ran the Flat Race, the Sack Race or the Grand Steeple-Chase.

One of Mount St Mary's sporting priests may have given Charlie the small booklet later handed down to Larry Wordsworth, my grandfather's cousin. Bound in dark red leather with Charlie's initials embossed in gold on the cover, the booklet is a kind of keep-fit cum magic manual, entitled *Indian Clubs, Dumb-Bells, and Sword Exercises*. Inside there are drawings of men in togas brandishing weapons, and much talk of fruit: 'Severing the Lemon on the Naked Hand', 'Cutting an Apple Inside a Silk Handkerchief Without Injuring the Latter' and 'Cutting the

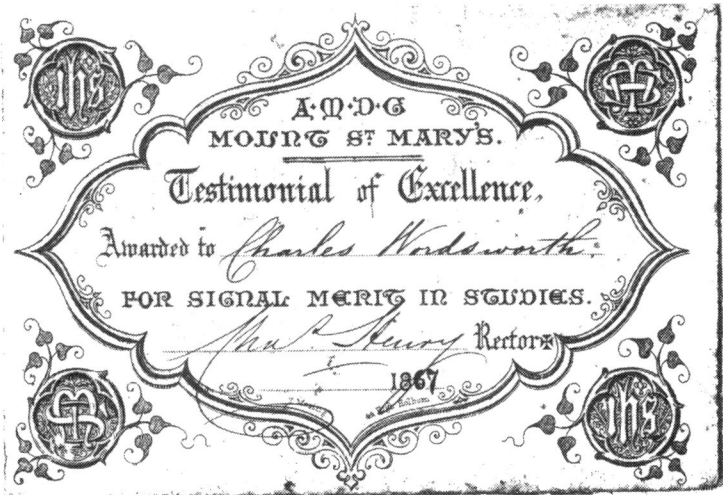

The certificate awarded to fifteen-year-old Charlie, retained for the rest of his life

Orange Under the Naked Peel'.

Whatever Charlie's prowess with the Indian Sword, academically he settled into the school well. In his fourth year, at the age of fifteen, he was awarded a 'Testimonial of Excellence for Signal Merit in Studies'. He kept this certificate for the rest of his life, and perhaps was proud of it.

Unlike his father, Charlie did not go on to Edinburgh University, or apprentice himself to a lawyer in the New Town. He did not have Samuel's connections, and perhaps felt his Catholicism would hinder him — the university was as staunchly Protestant as Edinburgh's legal and commercial worlds, and things were much the same in England.

Whatever his reasons for leaving Britain, Charlie Wordsworth was determined to migrate. By early 1875 he'd sailed out to New Zealand and returned already, and was now preparing to depart with his mother on the *Strathmore*. If he was looking for adventure, he would get it.

Black Jack Warren, Able Seaman

No mystery surrounds Black Jack Warren's decision to sail for New Zealand. He was a seaman in pursuit of his trade — he embarked on the *Strathmore* as part of the job. But like Charlie, Jack had been out to the colony already. Before boarding the *Strathmore* he served on the *Tweed*, shipping immigrants and iron to Otago.

If his reasons for making another New Zealand voyage are clear enough, almost everything else about him remains mysterious. He left few traces — just his entry in the *Strathmore's* crew list and several brief mentions in the survivors' testimony. A man assembled from the slightest of scraps, Black Jack seems a fit incarnation of the half-remembered past. Even his name does the job: Black for the night-time of the unknowable; Jack for Jack Tar, the sailors' everyman.

An Irishman from Belfast, at thirty-one Black Jack was by all accounts the popular leader of the *Strathmore* sailors. Young apprentice Harold Turner called him 'the man who was the chief' — 'and a capital ruler he made too', according to Charlie Wordsworth.

Turner said Jack was named for his 'very swarthy complexion'. He may have had Spanish or African heredity, but more likely, with the name Warren, this Ulsterman was a Protestant of English stock, a descendant of the tenant farmers who were planted on confiscated Catholic land in the seventeenth century.

By 1844, when John 'Black Jack' Warren was born, Belfast, his hometown, was a major seaport, known for ship-building, rope-making, linen, tobacco and whiskey. Though more prosperous than other parts of Ireland, still wages were low, poverty endemic and the town stank of bad drains.

It was just before the start of the great potato famine. Chances are Jack's father was a sailor, his mother a linen-mill worker. Many seafaring families lived in the densely crowded Dock District, later Sailortown, where houses clustered around tiny courts tucked between the main streets in a maze of crooked and often flooded laneways. Most houses had four rooms — two up, two down — and were shared by two families, as many as eighteen or twenty people.

Water was fetched from a public fountain, or a pump shared with neighbours, or from water carts. Many houses had no toilet facilities and 'nuisances' were often left on the streets until removed by the police carts. Potatoes and oatmeal were the staple food, occasionally supplemented by bread, herrings, buttermilk and pork or bacon.

In 1847, 1131 cases of fever were reported in the Dock District and papers published news daily of famine-related deaths in the streets of Belfast. In 1849 cholera broke out, and in 1851, when Jack was seven, the average age of those dying from the disease was just nine years old.

Street fighting and riots were common in the town during Jack's childhood.

Belfast's a famous northern town,
Ships and linen its occupation;
And the workers have a riot on
The slightest provocation.

Children joined in with enthusiasm — newspapers recorded 'urchins of ten to twelve years', 'boys and girls' and 'juvenile hooligans' among the rioters. Many skirmishes were related to Protestant–Catholic tensions, but fighting was intimately connected with Belfast's culture of heavy drinking. Whiskey was cheap, public houses plentiful and brawls often peaked after pay-time on Saturdays.

In the summer of 1857, unusually violent and prolonged riots bordered on warfare, forcing occupants of the Pound and Sandy Row areas — just blocks west of the Dock District — to leave their homes. But by 1857 Jack was thirteen, old enough to go to sea, and perhaps already had left Belfast.

Nineteenth-century ship's boys were employed as ordinary seamen, but they were paid much less than grown men — the *Strathmore* boys got just one pound a month. As ship's boy, young Jack would have done the jobs no-one else wanted, ranging from the menial — scrubbing decks and emptying latrines — to the perilous, such as going aloft in squalls to furl skysails and royals. 'Going aloft' — the phrase conjures an airy, balloon-like experience. But what did it mean to Jack in practice, on a dark and stormy night?

He would be ordered to climb a mast eight storeys high, by means of swaying rope ladders, the ship rolling and plunging in the dark, a gale driving rain into his face. The higher Jack climbed, the more the slippery rope ladders would narrow. When he finally reached the yard (the wooden spar suspended from the mast that spreads the top of a square-sail), the great sails would be thrashing and thwacking in the wind, threatening to knock him into the sea. Standing on a swinging rope, Jack would reach over the yard, also swinging and swaying from side to side, catch the sodden sail with his frozen fingers and roll it up tight. The job needed both hands — there was no way he could hold on with one hand and furl with the other.

An experienced sailor could easily lose his grip or miss his footing up in the rigging, but boys were even more vulnerable to death by falling — they were smaller, less skilled and more likely to be given such dangerous tasks by mates and masters unwilling to risk the lives of their able seamen. And when boys did go overboard, they were less likely to be picked up — many captains were reluctant to turn back a ship for the sake of a boy.

Black Jack's life would have become easier when he turned able seaman, but not much. The work was hard and the hours punishing — four hours on and four hours off, six or seven days a week.

On each voyage, Jack would be assigned to one of two watches — either the port watch, also called the first mate's watch, or the starboard or captain's watch. When on duty, he and his watch-mates were constantly busy: making and setting sail, reefing, furling, bracing, steering and keeping lookout. There was always tarring, greasing, oiling, varnishing, painting, scraping and scrubbing to be done, as well as the never-ending task of examining, adjusting and repairing the rigging. Strictly speaking the men were not supposed to talk to each other on deck, though no doubt they did if the officers were out of earshot.

After Jack's watch had done their four-hour stint, the off-watch came on duty while he and his mates had their 'watch below'. In the late afternoon there were two two-hour 'dog watches', which ensured that each group of men switched schedules after twenty-four hours, and that everyone ate their evening meal at a decent hour — the last dog-watchmen eating before going on duty at six, the first dog-men after knocking off at six. This timetable meant that at any given time on board ship someone was trying to get some sleep. Among the other noises that would-be sleepers had to contend with were the half-hourly bells regulating the watches.

Years of Jack's life were spent in this strange, highly regulated pattern: working furiously, sleeping and waking at all hours (perhaps suffering side effects such as headache, mood swings, fatigue and gastrointestinal trouble). Working conditions were often appalling — rotten food, brutal physical discipline and verminous quarters were all commonplace at sea. On board most ships Jack and his fellow sailors received a daily grog ration of rum and water — roughly three standard drinks, enough to warm a man up without getting him too drunk to work. Like many others Jack lived up to the image of the hard-drinking sailor, relying on alcohol as a source of comfort, enjoyment and escape.

Life at sea was hard, but perhaps not so bad when compared to life ashore. At least Jack could rely on getting fed and paid, however poorly, and on the company of his mates and a place to sleep. Also, he always had something to look forward to — the time in between voyages, release from the four-hourly revolving schedule of shipboard life into sudden freedom on shore, with money in his pockets and time on his hands. No doubt Jack and his mates frequented the sailors taverns, spending their wages on drink, beef dinners and prostitutes — sex being a source of comfort, enjoyment and escape more readily available on shore.

Did Black Jack have children? Did he marry? Did he send money home? Did he have a happy time of it with women? It's hard to say whether the sailors' life of extreme contrasts and long absences made men less likely to marry or form lasting loves or put their marriages and love affairs under increased strain. Arguably they were more likely to father children by multiple women, certainly a potential cause of marital strife. But perhaps such scenarios were not frequent, or anyway not frequently discovered.

Like many seamen Jack was only semi-literate, which compounded the difficulty of staying in touch with family during long voyages, though surely the most important communication was the reliable handing over of wages. As long as the money got home somehow (tricky, if there was more than one home to send it to), conjugal trouble was perhaps more likely when sailors were ashore too long, getting under the feet of families used to independence.

Heavy drinking can put strain on a marriage, and Jack could certainly drink. But if he was as generous and good-tempered with his family as with his mates, and if he was a steady drinker who sometimes binged rather than a constant drunk, his drinking may not have been a problem.

At any rate, by the time Black Jack Warren shipped on the *Strathmore* he was a skilled and respected sailor, a well-travelled man, one of the older members of the crew. Though a poor reader, he could sign his name and his sharp eyesight made him a good lookout.

His eyes and hair were dark, his skin tanned and weather-beaten. Neither remarkably big nor remarkably small, he was a dominant man, a leader, not afraid to threaten violence or back up his threats with his fists. He was not overly interested in following rules.

He spoke with an Ulster accent, likely sounding his Rs and saying some of his Ts as Ds. When he said 'later' it sounded like 'laderr', and his 'sort out' was more of a 'sorrd out'. Probably he had the Irish habit of avoiding 'yes' and 'no', preferring 'I have', 'I am', or 'I have not', 'I am not'.

'Thoroughly good-natured' to both Catholics and Protestants, in Turner's words Black Jack was 'as generous as any sailor who ever stepped aboard ship' — a man whom other men looked up to and liked to be around. No doubt he enjoyed a story and a laugh.

Wattie Walker, Child

Like Black Jack, little Wattie Walker made no decision to change his life in sailing for the colonies — he was too young to understand emigration, let alone choose it for himself. But his mother and father were going out to New Zealand, and naturally they took Wattie with them.

Long sea voyages were hard on children in the nineteenth century. They caught scarlet fever, measles, whooping cough and diphtheria. They fell overboard and drowned. They were killed in fires and wrecks.

Wattie was about two and a half when he boarded the *Strathmore* in April 1875. Safely past the most vulnerable age, Wattie was travelling saloon (or first) class with his parents; there was no nurserymaid, no sisters or brothers. According to the passenger list, his mother, Alice, was twenty-six years old; her occupation, 'Wife'. Like Charlie, Alice's 32-year-old husband, Alfred Walker, was listed as a 'Gent' — he worked as a sharebroker. Wattie was down as Walter A. H. Walker, his 'Profession, Occupation, or Calling: Child'.

He was not the only child on board, though the others were all in steerage, the eight sons and daughters of Elizabeth and Edward Goodrich: Frederick, Elizabeth, Rebecca, Hester Jane, Edward, Bertie, Florence and Louisa. Florence was the same age as Wattie, Louisa a year younger. Five-year-old Bertie probably thought himself a big boy, and was old enough to be annoyed by his little sisters. He would not get much chance to be annoyed by Wattie. Third-class passengers were not allowed in the saloon or cabins, and first-class ladies like Alice did not visit steerage, much less allow their children to venture below decks alone.

Wattie and his parents were from fast-growing Birmingham, the 'city of a thousand trades', 'workshop of the world'. People and goods flowed in and out of the Midlands town on canal boats and steam trains. At night the streets were lit by gas lamps and by day were full of carts, carriages and horse-drawn trams.

Birmingham was second only to London in population, and most of its children lived in overcrowded, badly built back-to-back houses. They spent their days on the streets, in school or in the town's many small manufacturing workshops, churning out buttons and cutlery, toys and guns, locks and screws and nails and tools. Just blocks away from the workshops and slums were large comfortable houses with piped water, carpeted staircases and nurseries full of rocking horses and Noah's arks for middle-class children like Wattie.

Clues to Wattie's daily life appear in *The Englishwoman's Domestic Magazine*, in articles such as the September 1872 issue's 'Physical Treatment of Children' and 'Babies, and How to Take Care of Them', which appeared in November 1877.

'When nurse is in the house,' the magazine instructed, 'it is generally the wisest plan to let her manage her young charge as she likes … unless she is detected in anything flagrantly wrong in her dealings with your child, do not interfere with her.' Advice was given to mothers, however, as 'Every woman, old or young, gentle or simple, ought to know something about the proper treatment of babies …'

So mothers were exhorted to give children 'plenty of exercise in the open air' — a rather sooty substance in 1870s Birmingham. Daily baths were recommended, 'in almost cold water', while children 'should eat regularly and simply … Bread and milk, bread and butter, different forms of toasted bread, simple preparations of corn flour, rice boiled in milk, and roasted potatoes, make a sufficient variety.' The importance of regular sleeping and eating hours was stressed, and eating between meals discouraged — 'it is of no use to get up elaborate rules for the punctuality of his meals if you allow him to be continually eating between them'.

Middle-class children were largely confined to second-floor nurseries, and wheeled in perambulators to the park every day before dinner. It was a life built around routine. A visit downstairs to the drawing room to meet company was an occasion, as was a father's visit to the nursery. Fathers were generally not seen for more than an hour or so each day, and the world was ruled by nurserymaids and mothers.

According to Charlie Wordsworth, Wattie Walker was 'a lively little child, and talked on board the ship'. His still downy hair was probably worn long. Too young to be breeched, he would have run about in woollen smocks or dresses dyed in bright, rich colours: puce, plum, scarlet, navy. Perhaps his limbs were still supple and squirmy in the way of little boys before they stiffen their bodies into the armour of grown men. Perhaps his high child's voice was not always easy to understand.

Wattie would be the only child to live through the wreck of the *Strathmore*. He would not have an easy time of it.

2

Voyage

As long as one and a half Olympic swimming pools laid end to end, as broad as six tall men laid head to foot — that's the size of the 74- by 11-metre iron-hulled sailing ship *Strathmore*, that was to house eighty-eight people on their three-month voyage from England to New Zealand. A brand-new ship in 1875, the *Strathmore* was built in Dundee for David Bruce's Dundee Clipper Line. The busy colonial trade meant a strong demand for new ships; before she was even launched, the *Strathmore* was chartered by Shaw Savill & Co to carry freight and migrants to Otago in New Zealand's South Island.

The Shaw Savill & Co shipping line began in the early days of the New Zealand gold-rush, seventeen years before the *Strathmore* was built, and by 1875 had a virtual monopoly on the New Zealand trade. The first notice of the *Strathmore's* maiden voyage appeared in *The Times* of 20 January, buried halfway down a timetable of New Zealand voyages listing sixteen different ships scheduled to sail during March, April and May 1875. The advertisement contained no details of what the *Glasgow Herald* three days later called the 'well and substantially built' *Strathmore's* 'smart and handsome appearance', of her cabins painted in the colours of oak, maple and rosewood, nor of her state-of-the-art machinery, including patent steering gear, windlass, steam winch and condenser. She and the other fifteen ships were described only collectively as 'first-rate passenger packets, fitted and equipped on plans founded upon long experience'. The accommodation and diet of the passengers, whatever their class, was not mentioned.

As befitted a first-rate passenger packet, the *Strathmore* was classed by Lloyd's Register of Shipping as 100A1. Then, as now, Lloyd's Register set standards for ship construction to help insurers assess the risk of indemnifying a ship against loss on the high seas. A 100A1 classification meant that Lloyd's approved a full set of plans for the *Strathmore*, that their surveyors had regularly inspected her during and after construction, and that they agreed she was a sound ship.

On 22 January 1875, two days after the appearance of that first *Times* advertisement, the *Strathmore* was launched from the yard of the Dundee shipbuilders Brown and Simpson by Jeannie

The good ship Strathmore, *as painted by C.K. Mitchell in 1875, lying in the Tay River off Broughty Ferry*

Smith, daughter of one of the twenty-seven Scottish merchants who formed the Dundee Clipper Line. Jeannie was standing in for the busy Earl of Strathmore, whose white-painted effigy adorned the ship's prow, and who cancelled his attendance when the launch was postponed due to the tides.

A crowd of carpenters, ship owners, women and children gathered around the new ship. Speeches were made, Jeannie broke a bottle over the newly painted bow and the crowd cheered as the *Strathmore* slid down the ways and into the water.

A first-rate passenger packet

Close readers of Shaw Savill & Co's 1875 *Times* advertisements would have observed, below the list of New Zealand departure dates, a brief note: 'To be obtained from [Shaw, Savill and Co] the 12th edition of the *New Zealand Handbook*, with supplement, post free, 1 shilling.'

Interested parties who sent in their shilling (more than a day's wages for a ship's boy on the *Strathmore*) received a copy of the *Handbook of Information for Passengers*, a small booklet crammed with detail on such diverse subjects as 'The Route', 'Baggage', 'Piano Fortes', 'Dietary', 'Engagement of Passages' and 'What a Man can "do" in New Zealand'.

Although I am more than a hundred and thirty years too late to purchase a Shaw Savill passage to Wellington, I feel a definite excitement as I turn the *Handbook*'s brittle, yellowing pages. Tourist-style propaganda mingles with terse instructions: 'The accommodation is excellent, situated in the tween-decks', 'the utopia of invalids and sightseers', 'CAUTION: Passengers are not allowed …', 'Ample room for ten times the present population', 'well-furnished with every requisite in shape of Bedding, Linen, Towels', 'no goods of a dangerous or damaging nature', 'penalty £100 plus damages' and so on.

The effect is simultaneously thrilling and reassuring — the promise of adventure backed by guarantees of order and comfort. My excitement is made more ridiculous by the fact that I am already *in* Wellington, sitting in the Alexander Turnbull Library Manuscripts Room. But still I feel it as I leaf through the booklet — the adrenaline of anticipation.

Near the front of the *Handbook* on a fold-out map of New Zealand, a long double-headed arrow approaches the country from the west, dashes between its North and South Islands and continues inexorably eastwards, off to the far edge of the paper. The western end of the arrow is labelled 'Route from London to Wellington via Cape of Good Hope'.

One of the most detailed sections of the *Handbook* is that headed 'Dietary', in which voyagers were told that Shaw Savill & Co's cuisine was 'unsurpassed by that of any line in the world'. The different fare offered to each class of passenger was summarised: 'The Saloon Table is of the most ample and elaborate kind, and will be found to satisfy the most fastidious tastes … Second Class also get a free and excellent table, the dishes supplied to them, although not so numerous as the Saloon Table, being of similar quality. Third Class passengers have a full supply of the best provisions …'

A table listed the weekly quantities of foodstuffs supplied to passengers: a pound of Preserved Meats, half a pound of York Ham, a quarter pound of Fish, a pound each of Prime India Beef and Irish Mess Pork, three and a half pounds of Biscuit. Diners could look forward to Sugar (Raw), Lime Juice (in Tropics), Potatoes (fresh or preserved), and Currants (or Raisins, Valencia), as well as Flour, Rice, Oatmeal, Barley, Tea, Coffee, Butter, Cheese, Suet, Mustard, Pepper, Salt and Pickles. 'We find it best for our own interest,' confided the *Handbook*, 'as well as for our passengers, to conduct our sea house-keeping … on a somewhat liberal scale.'

While prospective passengers were assured that shipboard provisions would 'be found fully adequate to supply all necessaries, and to keep up health and strength for even the longest voyage', those with children were advised that 'a few little extras will be found a nice addition to the sea-fare'. Jams and jellies, fancy biscuits, sago, arrowroot and raspberry vinegar were recommended — 'such like things as can be packed in small compass, and prepared without much trouble. Preserved milk, also, is a great, though rather an expensive, luxury ... Where there are children, it will be found a very nice thing.' No doubt Alice Walker, Wattie's mother, took note.

The baggage section is also detailed. Forty cubic feet (1.13m³) of baggage were allowed in first class, fifteen cubic feet (0.42m³) in steerage. Packages required in the cabin were not to exceed two feet six inches long, one foot broad and twelve inches deep (76cm x 30.5cm x 30.5cm). (Don't ask about the difference between one foot and twelve inches!) To avoid 'considerable inconvenience', these packages were to be labelled 'Cabin'. Other packages were to be labelled either 'Wanted On Voyage' or 'Not Wanted On Voyage', and were to be on board at least two days prior to departure.

All packages had to be strong, and could be insured against marine loss. Baggage could be collected from any address in and around London, 'at uniform rates', by the London Parcels Delivery Company.

Passengers were advised to pack warm heavy clothing for chilly sea breezes, and light thin clothing for use in the warmer latitudes, and they 'should provide sufficient linen to last the voyage, as no regular washing is done on board'.

Midway through the *Handbook of Information* is a copy of a letter purporting to be from two brothers travelling third class.

A breezy note, it begins with their surprise at the extreme cleanliness of the ship, and progresses through a brisk timetable of passing ports. References to singing and dancing, and phrases such as 'Monday commenced sports and amusements' and 'enjoyed ourselves immensely' contribute to the general impression that the voyage felt more like three days at a seaside resort than three months at sea.

The passengers' correspondent was informed that it was hot near the equator, 'but not uncomfortable', and that, though the ship had a 'rather rough time coming through the Indian Ocean', there was nevertheless 'nothing to be alarmed at'. Any alarm that might have been indulged in was soothed away by the attentions of the staff — 'nothing you asked for was too much trouble'.

On arrival in New Zealand the helpful crew garnered further approval by refusing to obey a notice to go on strike. Wellington was a 'very pretty place' with 'everything English about it'. Wages were good; shops opened till six. All in one brief sentence our friends got their boxes on shore, found 'respectable lodgings' and proceeded to the registry office where both brothers were hired 'on the spot, to start Monday morning'.

The rest of the *Handbook* is devoted to praise of New Zealand, which was characterised as 'a land where merit is the sole passport to success' and where the climate was 'most healthful and pleasant': 'Its temperature varies from that of the South of England to that of the South of Italy. Its cold is not so cold as that of any part of Ireland, and its warmth renders it the home of the orange, vine, fig and watermelon, which grow and ripen in the open air.'

Prospective migrants are told of cheap, plentiful food, good government, an egalitarian society and generous wages for all those willing and able to work. No mention is made of the very recent land wars; the Māori inhabitants of New Zealand — much feared by potential settlers — are referred to only briefly as a diminishing population. Surviving Māori are described as olive-skinned 'natural orators' who 'easily adapt themselves to European customs', have 'wonderful memories' and whose gestures, 'when not under warlike excitement', are 'graceful and dignified'.

Further reassurance is provided in the form of statistics. There are export figures for wool, tallow, sheepskins, timber, coal, flour, oatmeal, hops, butter, cheese, bacon, hams, salt beef and salt pork. There are census figures for European settlers, and also for sheep, horses, horned cattle, land under cultivation, letters received and despatched, miles of railway and scholars at public schools.

Finally, there is a quote from Professor Strong, LLD, formerly of Liverpool.

> New Zealand has the very extraordinary power of causing all who have once set foot on her shores to pass beneath the indescribable spell of her witchery. I never met anyone who, having tasted life in his new island home, would consent to change his abode. It is very hard to analyse this magic power of the beautiful gem of the Antipodes ... Nature has given all her charms to New Zealand, and keeps them as fresh and imperiously beautiful as Cleopatra's.

Assembling one's colonial outfit was quite an undertaking. Perhaps Fanny Wordsworth did some of her shopping in Edinburgh, at Roderick McLeod, Boot & Shoe Manufacturer of 65 North Hanover Street, 'where Every Description of Boots and Shoes that a Family Requires are Stocked in the Greatest Variety'. There she could choose between Sateen Elastic Boots, Morocco

Dressing Slippers and Cashmere Double-Buttoned Boots, and buy a Button Hook to wrangle her boots on and off.

Around the corner at 16 George Street, P & R Wright, Linen Manufacturers and Drapers, offered White Cotton Hose, Rib-knit Woollen Hose, Fingering Yarn, Linen Cuffs and Fancy Cambric Handkerchiefs. Perhaps Fanny bought White Turkish Towels, Night Gowns (plain, frilled or tuck-trimmed), Flannel Petticoats, a Flannel Dressing Gown, Chemises and Drawers.

If Fanny and Charlie heeded the *Handbook of Information*, they made at least some of their purchases in London: 'We should … advise all passengers to obtain the sea-going portion of their Outfit from one or other of the many respectable outfitters in London, for these Houses have had much experience in the trade …'

The *Handbook* counselled Fanny to equip herself with items including '1 good warm cloak (made with a hood), or 1 good warm shawl' plus '2 good flannel petticoats' and '6 pairs stockings (half worsted)'. Charlie was told to get '1 Scotch or other cap, and a southwester or good felt hat' and warned against 'Chimney-pot hats' which 'are not worn on board, nor yet in the colony'. They would both need '4 towels, and 2 lbs marine soap' for the voyage.

Once outfitted, the Wordsworths had friends and family to visit. They said goodbye to Fanny Rosamund and her husband, and perhaps made a trip to Tunbridge Wells to see Fanny's sister, Mrs Elizabeth Wood. It may have been this round of farewells that had led them to choose the *Strathmore* from Shaw Savill & Co's timetable of New Zealand voyages. The *Earl of Zetland*, another new ship, was to sail ten days earlier, the *Blair Gowrie* a month later. The first of March — the *Strathmore*'s advertised embarkation date — must have seemed a convenient time.

As the *Handbook of Information* observed, 'the *earlier* cabins and berths are secured … the better the choice'. Did the Wordsworths listen to this advice, posting the half-price deposit for two *Strathmore* tickets (a bank draft for about fifty guineas) to the Shaw Savill office by early February? If so, their plans would be mucked about four times over the next two and a half months — Shaw Savill's advertisements may have resembled a timetable of voyages to New Zealand, but it was not a timetable that ran with any precision.

On 8 February the *Strathmore*'s embarkation was postponed until 10 March. Eleven days later this became 20 March. By 3 April, the ship had still not sailed. A final advertisement listed the *Strathmore*'s departure as 10 April, though she did not sail for another week after that.

In March, the month initially planned for her departure, the *Strathmore* was still in Dundee, being 'swung' — rotated about a fixed point while her orientation was noted against landmarks on shore. Mr Peter Feathers adjusted her three compasses, using magnets to correct error. 'They were all in good order,' he said later, 'and as well-placed as they could be.' He noted that the magnetism of the ship's large cast-metal steering apparatus affected the wheel compass, and would 'tend to make the error of the compass a little erratic' at latitudes beyond Dundee.

After making his corrections, Mr Feathers issued a certificate and a skeleton crew sailed the *Strathmore* down to London. Over two thousand tons of cargo were loaded at the East India Dock, including salt, wax matches, cement, earthenware, coals, railway tracks, brandy, rum, wine, beer and 'Geneva Liquor', or gin. Mr Feathers commented later that if he'd known so much iron was to be stowed in the mainhold — 111 tons of iron rails and 300 tons of wrought-iron bars — he would have recommended that the ship be re-swung.

The voyage begins

Up in Birmingham, it is likely, Wattie was getting new clothes. Did he stand still while his mother pinned the hems on his dresses? *Stop fidgeting, turn around, just a minute ...*

Luggage would have begun to collect in the Walkers' downstairs hallway: an ever-growing pile of great parcels and tin trunks towering over Wattie. *What are they for, why are they there? Where are we going? What is New Zealand?*

In a less salubrious part of the world, Shadwell in London's East End, Black Jack Warren and his mate Old Jack Evans would have set off for the Shaw Savill shipping office at 34 Leadenhall Street some time in March or early April. They were going there to sign the 'Agreement and Account of Crew (Foreign-Going Ship) No. 8537', covering the *Strathmore's* maiden voyage from London to Otago and back again, 'to a final port of discharge in the United Kingdom. Voyage not to exceed two years.' They were advanced a month's wages: three pounds, five shillings.

Evans signed first, then Black Jack took the pen and wrote his name — John Warren — in a firm and careful copperplate with flamboyant capitals. The two men were the first able seamen to sign the agreement. It required them to obey the captain's commands and 'conduct themselves in an orderly, faithful, honest and sober manner, and to be at all times diligent in their respective Duties'. They were promised a 'daily issue of Lime and Lemon Juice', a daily pound of bread (about half a loaf) and a pound and a half of beef four times a week. Thrice weekly they were to get a pound and a quarter of pork, a quarter-pint of peas and a half-pound of flour, with 'Substitutes as Comfort or Necessity may require'.

To get from their lodgings in Shadwell to the *Strathmore's* berth at the East India Dock in Blackwall, Black Jack and Old

Jack had to walk through the Limehouse district. Shadwell, Limehouse and Blackwall were maritime neighbourhoods, with sizable communities of South Asian, Chinese, African and Greek seamen. There were opium dens and breweries, shipbuilders and ship's chandlers. Writer Henry Mayhew described the area in 1851.

> *The courts and alleys ... swarm with low lodging-houses ... inhabited either by the dock-labourers, sack-makers, watermen, or that peculiar class of the London poor who pick up a living by the water-side. The open streets themselves have all more or less a maritime character. Every other shop is either stocked with gear for the ship or the sailor. The windows of one house are filled with quadrants and bright brass sextants, chronometers, and huge mariners' compasses ... their cards trembling with the motion of the cabs and wagons passing in the street. Then comes the sailors' cheap shoe-mart, rejoicing in the attractive sign of 'Jack and his Mother'. Every public-house is a 'Jolly Tar', or something equally taking. Then come sailmakers, their windows stowed with ropes and lines smelling of tar. All the grocers are provision-merchants, and exhibit in their windows ... cases of meat and biscuits; and every article is warranted to keep in any climate. The corners of the streets, too, are mostly monopolised by slopsellers; their windows part-coloured with bright red-and-blue flannel shirts; the doors nearly blocked up with hammocks and 'well-oiled nor'-westers'; and the front of the house itself nearly covered with canvas trousers, rough pilot-coats, and shiny black dreadnoughts. The passengers alone would tell you that you were in the maritime districts of London. Now you meet a satin-waistcoated mate, or a black sailor with his large fur cap, or else a Custom-house officer in his brass-buttoned jacket.*

No doubt the two Jacks were known at some of the Limehouse pubs — the Grapes maybe, or the Devil's Tavern. Their last chance for a drink ashore was early on Saturday, 17 April. Later that fine spring morning, as the *Strathmore* moved away from the crowded Blackwall Pier, a drunken sailor — Black Jack, perhaps — jumped aboard from the dockhead amid the cheering and waving of the onlookers yelling goodbye.

A tugboat towed the ship down the Thames, past Canning Town, Woolwich and Creekmouth. In the early afternoon she passed Gravesend and was moored two miles downriver, where a lighter came alongside her, carrying twelve tons of gunpowder. Black Jack and the other sailors lugged the barrels down the main-hatch and stacked them between decks on an old sail. There was no iron lining round the so-called gunpowder room, just stacks of wooden cases; the *Strathmore* was permitted to ship explosives with no powder magazine because she did not carry enough passengers to fall under the Passenger Act. When all the barrels were stowed, the men drew the sail up over them and made it fast. Then they fastened and caulked the hatch, filling the cracks with oakum to make it watertight.

Though most second-class and all steerage passengers boarded ship in London, saloon passengers embarked at Gravesend. 'To save themselves expense,' counselled the *Handbook of Information*, 'fore cabin passengers from the country, after they have all ready to start, should write and ask us what day they must be at the docks.'

Up in Birmingham, Wattie Walker saw the last of his nurserymaid — some Meg or Sally, Annie or Flo, the young woman who'd taken care of him for longer than he could remember. The little boy would have made his final journey down the stairs, along the now-empty hallway and out the front door, before being handed up into a cab and settled on his mother's knee. Off they would have jolted, trotting through the streets to the clatter and roar of New Street Station, light glaring through the massive vaulted glass roof, great trains hissing and clanking.

The Walkers travelled down to London on the Great Western Railway. After their arrival at Paddington Station his father would have hailed a cab to Fenchurch Street, where the family was to catch the Gravesend train. For Wattie, whose days had been so simple, so orderly, everything had changed. For the first time in his short life his nurse was gone, her familiar presence replaced by Father — rough-faced, deep-voiced, tobacco-breathed and almost a stranger.

In Father's arms he would have been carried up the steps of the train, out of the echoing din and into a first-class compartment full of strange grown-ups. The train would have rattled and roared as it began to move. Jiggling and swaying on his mother's knee, perhaps Wattie gazed out the window at the world rushing past: the station platform, the station yard, the streets of Birmingham, the countryside. Tickets would be clipped, sandwiches eaten. Surely Wattie slept. Then another noisy station, another jolting cab, a night spent in strange lodgings, more stations, more cabs and finally the Walkers arrived at Gravesend — the wharf, the smell of the river.

The *Handbook of Information* cautioned passengers to be wary about the waterside, instructing them to 'give the cold shoulder to any strangers who may kindly offer to assist them in any little matter; for sometimes there are even decent-looking men prowling round the docks and dock streets, whose room is better than their company'.

The *Strathmore* was anchored about half a mile from the pier, but 'Shore boats put passengers on board,' advised the *Handbook*, 'at the rate of 6d. per head.' Wattie would have sat with his parents in the little boat, feeling it rock and glide with the motion of the oars and the current beneath him. Did he look down at the brown water and up at the immense ship, growing larger and nearer, tall masts towering into the sky?

By ten o'clock on the Monday night, when the crew weighed anchor and the *Strathmore* left Gravesend, moving down the Thames toward the ocean, Wattie, who had never seen the sea before, would have been fast asleep in his cabin. Perhaps the next morning he stood on deck holding his mother's hand, a little boy on a large ship made small by the wide waters of the English Channel.

The watches were picked when the ship got into the Channel. Black Jack was in the first mate's watch, along with a dozen others. There were six able seamen, including Darkey Fellows (who'd sailed with Jack on the *Tweed* the year before), the young Norwegian Hans Eriksen and an Irishman, Philip Cogan. There was also an eighteen-year-old ordinary seaman, Charles Tookey; the quartermaster, William Husband, known as Old Nimrod; the teenage apprentices Frankie Carmichael and Harold Turner; another ordinary seaman; and the third mate, John Crabb Allan.

For two days the ship was towed down the Channel to the Isle of Wight, where on Wednesday, 21 May, she hove to and waited while the cutter collected the pilot. This was the final chance for passengers and crew to send mail before leaving England. During the last-minute scribbling and sealing of envelopes, a brisk wind sent the ship pitching and rolling, turning the passengers' stomachs.

For Fanny Wordsworth, this was the beginning of over two months of fever and severe seasickness. 'I was sick the whole way,' she wrote, 'and if the sickness stopped, I had nausea.'

Confined to her cabin for weeks on end, she saw only the captain — who doctored her in the absence of a ship's surgeon

— her son, and eighteen-year-old Maggie Henderson, 'the lady who occupied the other berth in my cabin'. Lying in her narrow berth between bouts of vomiting, Fanny tried to sleep, or scratched her flea-bites, or simply fixed her eyes on the planks of the walls and ceiling, swallowing the bile that rose in her throat. 'I thought I should never reach New Zealand ...'

Up on deck, as the ship set sail after the pilot had gone, Charlie Wordsworth watched the Isle of Wight recede. His last sight of England was Start Point on the Devon coast, before the *Strathmore* left the Channel for what one of the third-class passengers called a 'quick and pleasant' run across the Bay of Biscay and out into the open sea.

Over the next week and a half the weather grew warmer as the ship sailed south. 'I could not eat,' wrote Fanny afterward. 'I loathed everything.'

Perhaps she took some coffee or tea when it was brought to the first-class cabins at six each morning. The 'everything' she loathed was served to her son, Charlie, and the hardier saloon passengers at the nine o'clock breakfast, the one o'clock luncheon, the four o'clock afternoon tea and the six o'clock dinner. 'Eating, drinking, and sleeping,' observed the *Handbook of Information*, 'occupy many an hour of the four-and-twenty ...'

Wattie's meals were just as frequent, but instead of the meat served to adults he got extra sago, bread, rice, raisins, suet and sugar. Up in the deckhouse, Black Jack and his watch-mates ate their salt beef and biscuits, washing them down with lime juice and tea.

On Monday, 3 May, the lookout man saw the islands of Madeira twelve miles off, at exactly the expected hour — the last land sighted from the *Strathmore*. The ship's compasses, at this stage, were accurate.

Not a fish to see

Long sea voyages can be very boring. There is no getting off
the boat, and once land disappears the view is always the same:
mile upon mile of ocean, stretching out in all directions to meet
the endless ring of the horizon. Even when a ship is moving
fast, the only real clue that she is getting anywhere is the long
unchanging line of her wake.

The *Strathmore* was not moving fast. Ever since leaving
the Channel, the winds had been either adverse or very light.
Eighteen days after passing Madeira, and a full fortnight after
she would have crossed the equator if she'd been making good
time, the ship was still three weeks away from the line.

'We are now only going from two to three knots an hour,'
wrote first-class passenger Thomas Henderson, 'and so steadily
that one can't perceive the motion of the vessel at all.'

Writing to her daughter via a passing ship on 21 May,
Fanny Wordsworth was feeling well enough to complain of
monotony. 'We have had a very tedious voyage as yet ... as for
enjoyment on board there is no such thing ... Some days not a
fish to see.'

Her ennui was not alleviated by the other female saloon
passengers — 'the two first-class ladies are worse than commonplace, underbred-women ... I distract mind and body from them
as much as possible.' Though Fanny evidently did not warm
to Wattie's mother, Mrs Walker, it was her cabin-mate, Miss
Henderson — the 'weak minded pretentious idiot' — who was
particularly irritating.

Perhaps Fanny's powers of forbearance were affected by the
heat. The weather was 'boiling hot', and she 'suffered terribly'.
On 20 May there was a 'fearful thunderstorm — such lightening
[sic] we have no idea of in England ... but I did not feel at all
afraid'.

'It rained in torrents at night,' recalled Charlie Wordsworth. 'All the young fellows got out on the poop & had a regular Bacchanalian dance & wash — in very light habiliments indeed — terrible lightning playing all the time.'

Fanny and the other ladies did not venture on deck during the storm, but Captain MacDonald described the scene to them afterwards. '[He] said it was like a ship of white savages in the gleams of lightening [sic],' reported Fanny. 'They have great fun,' she added wistfully. 'We poor women have a weary time of it.'

Fanny was one of only seven women on board the *Strathmore*. There were also nine children and seventy-two men, thirty-four of them passengers. Most migrant ships took over three hundred passengers during the great New Zealand bound exodus of the mid 1870s. But the space between the *Strathmore*'s decks was largely filled with cargo, leaving room for just fifty emigrants.

At a time when the majority of people moving to New Zealand were assisted migrants, their tickets subsidised by supporters in the colony, the *Strathmore* passengers paid their own fares. Though better off than most emigrants of the period, they probably left home for much the same reasons. By 1875 Britain had been in an economic slump, or at least a slowdown, for several years.

Country people suffered greatly from the agricultural downturn. As cheap colonial wheat lowered already plummeting prices, farm workers found their scant wages falling, their poor living conditions deteriorating, their jobs replaced by casual day labour or nothing at all. Rural refugees flocked to already overcrowded urban areas in search of work.

Cities and towns in Victorian Britain were notoriously unhealthy. Factory chimneys and coal fires filled the air with soot. Stomach-turning smells emanated from open sewers, tanneries, soap works and abattoirs. Fresh food was expensive and often scarce, and prepared food was frequently contaminated by poisons such as lead or strychnine, or fouled by human or animal excrement. Infected water caused hundreds of thousands of deaths from cholera and typhoid. In poorer districts two or three families shared single rooms, helping the spread of diseases such as tuberculosis. Many slept in the streets.

Though the *Strathmore* passengers were not poor, few town-dwellers could avoid the discomforts and dangers of pollution and poor sanitation, and many feared falling into the highly visible underclass. No social security existed in Victorian Britain, and illness or bad luck could easily send people into a downward spiral of penury and debt. Dread of poverty helped migrants brave the peril and monotony of the journey to New Zealand. Downplaying the peril, the *Handbook of Information* presented the monotony in a redemptive light: 'The voyage may seem, and really is, a long one … though in 80 or 100 days at sea there will be tedious hours, the reflective emigrant easily endures them when he remembers that emigration is a tonic medicine, saving or restoring us, and that the voyage it entails is the mere smack of bitter tasted for the moment as we take the draught.'

Thirty-two of the *Strathmore*'s fifty migrants were travelling steerage. The Goodriches and their eight children had joined the ship after leaving Botley, a village in Hampshire — on the run from what another third-class passenger called 'financial embarrassment'. A 27-year-old saleswoman, Sarah Jane Silk, was travelling with her younger brother, Francis, a land surveyor. The remaining twenty steerage passengers were single men — farmers, clerks, engineers, a mason, a grocer, a brewer, a miner, a shoemaker, a sea-captain's son. Most of them were in their twenties or even younger.

There were two single men in second class, along with two married couples, the Riddells and the Mabilles, who were returning to homes in New Zealand. Henrietta Mabille's husband, Theophilus, was an engineer; Mary Riddell's husband, James, was a farmer, as was 69-year-old James Blair. Like Charlie Wordsworth, 27-year-old Henry Sinnock was listed as a 'Gent'.

Charlie and Fanny were two of twelve first-class passengers. There was George D. Crombie, from the elegant middle-class London suburb of Stockwell; Frederick W. Bentley, also from London; and nineteen-year-old Hilton Keith, of unknown origin. The Joslen boys, a nineteen-year-old surveyor, Percy, and his brother, Spencer, were the sons of a Maidstone solicitor. Fanny's cabin-mate, Maggie Henderson, was travelling with her older brother, twenty-year-old Thomas, to meet their engineer father in Wellington. And then there was the Walker family: Alfred, Alice and Wattie.

The only record of Wattie at this period is Charlie's later memory of the 'lively little child, who talked on board ship'. At two-and-a-half Wattie would have been swiftly absorbing new words, stringing them together in short sentences. Perhaps he chattered to himself while falling asleep in the evenings, bedding down his latest vocabulary as he told himself the story of his day.

Was Wattie affected by the boiling heat which caused Fanny so much distress? Maybe it was easier to bear in a child's short dress than in a lady's high-necked gown. Certainly there was plenty to distract him from the temperature: new people, sights, sounds, smells — the endless fascinations of a ship at sea.

Some of Wattie's liveliness may have taken the form of tantrums, as the ordinary frustrations of a toddler longing for independence were heightened by the restrictions of shipboard life. How did his mother keep him from climbing the rigging and falling into the sea? Did she tie him to a rail? Keep him inside the family cabin or constantly in her arms? Divert him from danger with toys and games?

Perhaps the sailors entertained him. Fed up with weeks of calm and light winds, they might have enjoyed playing games with the children, making toys for their amusement. This may have been Wattie's first acquaintance with Yankee Bill Vining, an American sailor who was soon to become of great importance in the little boy's life. But perhaps Mrs Walker kept Wattie away from men like Yankee Bill, with his quick temper and habit of breaking into what one third-class passenger called 'a very torrent of cursing and blasphemy'.

If he got anywhere near the sailors, Wattie would have noticed their smell. He was used to women, and working men smelled very different — a rank, earthy odour of sweat and dirt, damp wool, rum and tobacco.

There were thirty-one men on the crew of the *Strathmore*, not counting officers and apprentice officers: eighteen able seamen, five ordinary seamen and eight petty officers — bosun, sailmaker, carpenter, three stewards, a cook and an engine driver. Most of the sailors were young — twelve were under the age of twenty-five, including three teenage boys, and all but five were under thirty-three. Over half were English, and over half the Englishmen were Londoners. There were also six Scotsmen, three Irishmen, three Scandinavians and two Americans.

They were, according to one third-class passenger, 'rather a rough lot'. A first-class passenger called them 'nasty, ill-conditioned', and the third mate said they were 'the worst lot I have ever seen'. The second steward described the sailors as 'very bad ... I do not think we could have had a worse lot ... very bad characters ... quarrelsome ... drunk ...' The ship's carpenter — who was perhaps closer to the sailors than the officers, stewards or passengers — gave a more favourable report: 'The crew behaved very well, except that once they were in drink for a few days.'

Fifteen-year-old apprentice Harold 'Farmer John' Turner was
an enthusiastic admirer of his crewmates' generosity and good
nature, preferring their society to that of the passengers: 'I never
met with a more selfish set of men than most of the passengers
were, they took care to look after number one.'

Fanny Wordsworth liked the sailors too. She praised their
courage, warm hearts and good spirits.

> ... the crew were all so kind to me...
>
> The men have... very hard work, and they do it all so
> cheerfully...
>
> Some of the men were great favourites of mine. Walter
> Smith or 'Sails,' [the sailmaker] as we always called him, was
> a gem in his way. He would knock down his enemy one minute,
> and the next risk his life for him, and when he had a friendship
> it was to the death; he was always so generous and kind — so
> were they all.

Kind, nasty, well-behaved, ill-conditioned, generous, quarrelsome,
loyal, rough and cheerful. Chances are the *Strathmore* sailors were
also rather short, by our standards — perhaps averaging around
163 centimetres. Their faces were surely tanned and weather-
beaten and most likely they wore short monkey jackets and
loose trousers over button-up vests, collarless shirts and woollen
stockings. Many were dirty and scruffy; passengers noted that
the *Strathmore*'s crew did not have the 'smart appearance' of
sailors on other ships.

They called each other 'lads' or 'boys', and went by
nicknames: Darkey, Daddy, Dutch Charlie, Farmer John, Jemmy
Duck, Yankee Bill, Big George, Black Jack, Old Jack, Young Jock,
Old Nimrod, Sails, Steam, Funny Lad. And they swore a lot,
uttering what one third-class passenger called their 'habitual

oaths' in Cockney, North Country, Scottish, Irish, American, Norwegian, Danish and Swedish accents.

They told stories and joked around, laughing about what made them anxious: over-refined manners, shipboard ignorance, cannibalism, the fear of death. They used humour and ridicule to cheer themselves up and to defuse tension and competitiveness. They were well-travelled men; they had seen many things. Most of them were not overtly religious, though their thoughts would turn to religion when they were afraid.

The 22-year-old ordinary seaman Tom Blackmore missed his father, with whom he worked before he went to sea. Able seaman Ted Sharp was a 29-year-old Cockney 'whose name and nature were the same', according to one passenger. Carpenter John Pirie was a shipwright for thirteen years but had never been to sea before. Eighteen-year-old Charles Tookey was in the habit of writing to his mother. Irishman Jemmy Duck had only one eye. Black Jack's mate Old Jack Evans had been shipwrecked several times. Big George once lived at the Cape of Good Hope, and Old Nimrod, the quartermaster, was known among the passengers as 'an inveterate grumbler'.

The regular crew of the *Strathmore* was kept apart from the officers by shipboard hierarchy, social class and the layout of the ship. Sailors and officers did not eat together. The crew's quarters were up forward — where the motion of the ship is the strongest — in the fo'c'sle, while the captain and mates had their quarters aft, and ate their meals in the saloon.

First-class passenger Thomas Henderson found the officers 'very agreeable' company, as did Fanny Wordsworth. She got on well with Captain MacDonald, who was 'exceedingly kind and attentive' to her. A 53-year-old Scotsman with a wife and family in Arbroath, MacDonald had been at sea about thirty years.

According to Fanny, he had 'great skill in medicine', for which she was deeply grateful.

While Fanny languished below decks, struggling with seasickness and fever, Charlie amused himself during the long voyage as best he could. 'There is company and conversation,' observed the *Handbook of Information*,

> *the weekly service of religion (when among our passengers there is no Minister of Religion to take Sunday morning Service, the Commander, or some obliging volunteer, reads prayers to all on board in the Chief Cabin, or in fine weather on the Poop), the solace of books, chess and draughts, evening song and occasional dance, the meeting of other travellers on the deep, the painted skies of tropical sunsets, and the novel sights of dolphin and boneta, nautilus and flying fish, albatross and frigate-bird, shark and whale.*

A keen amateur artist, Charlie may have been the passenger for whom one of the *Strathmore*'s boats was launched, so that he could sketch the ship. No lifeboat drills were held, and this was the only occasion on which any boat was launched during the voyage.

When the ship finally crossed the equator around 10 June, an unnamed small boy — either Wattie or five-year-old Bertie Goodrich — starred in the sailors' celebrations. Whether he took part or not, Wattie would have been enthralled. A trident-brandishing sailor descended from the fo'c'sle dressed as Neptune in tin crown and waist-length oakum beard, knickerbockers and one red and one white stocking. Six near-naked painted men pulled the god about the deck on a cart, with his oakum-haired transvestite wife nursing Wattie — or Bertie — on her knee.

Charlie Wordsworth, who had crossed the line before on that mysterious trip to Auckland, would have escaped the ritual shave and haircut, but Wattie's father might have undergone the ordeal. What did Wattie make of the spectacle? Two sailors dressed as policemen would have grabbed Father, that respectably whiskered and waistcoated stockbroker, and marched him over to the 'barber'. They would have held him down while he was lathered up, shaved with a rough piece of tin and had his hair hacked off with a pair of outsize blunt tin scissors. When the barber was finished, the men would have taken Father by the legs and thrown him backwards into a sail full of water, where he would have landed with a gigantic splash — no doubt setting Wattie giggling or shrieking with a mixture of glee and alarm.

Almost a mutiny

Some time in May, the *Strathmore* was partly swung — they 'could not swing her all round at sea,' said second mate Thomas B. Peters — and the compasses adjusted. Afterwards he could not remember whether this occurred north or south of the line. The ship was not swung again, nor were the compasses adjusted, as far as he knew.

The frequent calms and slight winds meant more slow and boring sailing. To add insult to dullness, the mild weather also deprived the *Strathmore*'s crew of their grog ration. 'The men only had it in bad weather,' said the second steward, 'when there was extra work.' The sailors were not allowed their own stores of drink either: 'No spirits are allowed' proclaimed a handwritten note near the bottom of the crew agreement.

According to the third mate, the men 'were showing signs of discontent and getting quarrelsome' as early as late April. They may have signed their names to the no-spirits rule, but weeks on end without a drink were too much for many of them, especially when they knew the mainhold was full of liquor. They'd stowed it themselves — casks of bulk spirits and beer, cases of gin, brandy and wine.

One hot night in May, the temptation became too much. Someone picked a lock, and Black Jack and his mates got down the fore hatches. Stumbling in the darkness round bulky barrels, boxes and bundles, the men climbed into an open space above the cargo and made their way to where the spirits were stowed. They took two or three cases of gin back to the fo'c'sle and began to drink.

Reports vary as to what happened next. Twenty men got drunk, or twelve — 'of whom one was the boson', according to an outraged third-class passenger — and they were incapable of work for three days, or for one. Passengers worked alongside the 'sober few of the crew' to sail the ship. According to Charlie Wordsworth there was 'great fighting & carrying on — almost a mutiny'. A passenger was among the drunken men. 'I had the honour of giving him two smart raps in the face,' Charlie wrote to his sister, 'which laid him in the scuppers.' The man was clapped in irons for swearing at the captain.

When the officers searched the fo'c'sle a day or two later, they could only find three bottles to confiscate. The captain did not inquire into how the men had taken the gin, and they were not punished, though ten names were entered in the ship's log, perhaps with a view to future prosecution, or at least cost recovery. 'Any Embezzlement or wilful or negligent destruction of the Ship's Cargo or Stores shall be made good to the Owner out of the Wages of the Person guilty of the same ...' proclaimed the crew agreement.

Despite complaining of the lack of excitement, Fanny Wordsworth did not mention the drunkenness or fighting in her letter to her daughter; the incident was no doubt less vivid in the minds of those who'd been below when it occurred.

3

Wreck

The *Strathmore* sailed down the map of the world, round the Cape of Good Hope and down below the southernmost tip of Africa, out of the Atlantic and into the Indian Ocean. Captain MacDonald was taking the Great Circle Route, dipping down into the Roaring Forties where the great winds could save a New Zealand-bound ship over a month of sailing. He plotted the *Strathmore*'s progress on the white-backed charts he kept on the table in his cabin, but away from the charts there was nothing to see — no land to give a sense of the journey, just water and waves, sky and horizon.

The weather was changing, growing steadily cooler as the ship headed south. Toward the end of June the *Strathmore* was sailing through rain, the skies too cloudy for the taking of observations. On Monday, 28 June, there was fog, which grew steadily thicker throughout that day and the next.

Wednesday, 30 June, was dull and drizzly, with a moderate south-west breeze and thick fog. Black Jack's day started at four am, scrambling out of his bunk in the fo'c'sle at the sound of the ship's bell — eight loud clangs — then into his boots and onto the damp deck for the morning watch. When he knocked off at eight it was beginning to get light; time for washing down a thick slab of bread with a mug of sweet tea before snatching an hour or two of sleep.

The first-class passengers had been roused at six by a gentle knock, the smell of fresh coffee or steeping tea drifting from the trays left by cabin doors. Fanny Wordsworth, of course, did not generally rise for nine o'clock breakfast but Charlie and Wattie were probably there, Wattie's mother spooning porridge into him, Charlie buttering his bread.

It was dull weather for Wattie, cooped up in the tiny cabin or the cramped saloon with little else but meals to break the day's monotony: luncheon at one, afternoon tea at four.

A sailor on the afternoon watch, possibly Black Jack, asked first mate Ramsay about some seaweed that was floating against the ship. 'We are near some islands,' said Ramsay, and gave orders to change the ship's course by half a point — no sights had been taken for three days and the captain wanted to keep well south of the Twelve Apostles, the northernmost islands of the treacherous Crozet Archipelago.

Black Jack ate his tea around five o'clock, while the men on the first dog watch shortened sail, a further precaution against the danger of the islands. The *Strathmore* had slowed to six knots, around 11 kilometres an hour, and would travel about 240 kilometres over the course of the day.

Feeling 'rather better', Fanny Wordsworth got up for dinner in the saloon. Captain MacDonald sat down with the passengers, congratulating Fanny on her rallying health and playfully threatening to 'land her on the Twelve Apostles' if she did not make a proper recovery soon. Wattie's bedtime would have been soon after dinner, but Fanny stayed up to play a game of cards — her first on board — before retiring to her cabin. She 'had generally slept badly hitherto, the fever always returning in the night', but not so that night — 'being more fatigued than usual, I slept soundly'.

During the evening, Captain MacDonald showed his chart to nineteen-year-old first-class passenger Percy Joslen, pointing out the Crozet Islands. He was wearing his oilskin, and told Joslen he would be on deck all night. They were then about eighty-seven miles from the Crozet Group, the captain said, but he talked of altering their course to make sure of clearing the rocks, as he was not exactly sure where the ship was. On his way to bed, Joslen told Charlie and the other young men in first class that he was not 'half-satisfied about the affair'. He even declared he would sleep in his clothes, but they laughed him out of the plan.

Charlie and Fanny and Wattie lay in their bunks as the *Strathmore* sailed on. At midnight Black Jack got up for the middle watch with the first mate and a dozen others. It was cold up on deck in the light south-west breeze and steady drizzle, the darkness made thicker by dense, soaking fog.

No more than a ship's length ahead

From midnight on Thursday, 1 July, eighteen-year-old ordinary seaman Charles Tookey was on lookout. 'The weather was very thick,' he said later. '[I] could not … [see] more than a ship's length ahead …'

At two o'clock in the morning he was relieved by Norwegian able seaman Hans Eriksen, three years his senior. Tookey went down into the fo'c'sle out of the rain and wind, along with Black Jack and the other men not needed on deck. They sat up yarning to keep themselves awake.

At 3.15, first mate Ramsay came to the fo'c'sle head and told Eriksen to keep a good lookout for the Crozet Islands. Half an hour later, Eriksen came down into the fo'c'sle saying he thought he'd seen land.

Hurrying out on deck, Black Jack heard it straight away: the dull rhythm of waves breaking on shore.

'Hard-a-starboard!' he yelled. 'Breakers right ahead!'

Far away near the back of the ship, the man at the wheel — bright-eyed little Darkey Fellows, Black Jack's old shipmate — did not hear.

Jack yelled again, louder: 'Hard-a-starboard!'

But first mate Ramsay was running forward from the poop. 'Hard-a-port! Port fore-brace! Let go the starboard braces!'

As he reached the fo'c'sle head, Ramsay corrected his own order: 'Hard-a-starboard! Starboard fore-brace!'

Jagged rocks loomed through fog on the starboard side as Black Jack and the other sailors began pulling the heavy yards round to change the ship's direction.

'She'll clear it, boys!' called the sailmaker.

And then the ship struck. Over four thousand tons of iron and timber, cargo and passengers smashed into serrated volcanic stone. Rock tore through the iron hull, first on the port side, then the starboard. Water surged into the lower hold, bursting open the 'tween-decks.

Within fifteen minutes, thirty-nine people would drown.

The ship has struck

Lying in her cabin, Fanny Wordsworth was woken by a series of jarring bumps: 'I was knocked violently backwards and forwards in my berth.'

The bumping was followed by 'a crunching and grating sound which could not be mistaken'. She and her young cabin-mate, Maggie Henderson, jumped out of bed.

We ... had just lit our lamps, when Charlie and Mr Henderson came to our cabin ...

'Mother, the ship has struck, and is quickly settling down. You have not time to dress — only a moment to put on what you can.'

They left us; we never spoke.

I helped the poor child to dress; she was pale and trembling, but quiet and collected. I did not take time to dress myself fully, merely putting on my dressing-gown and ... tweed tunic ... My sealskin jacket was unfortunately locked up, so I huddled on my warm shawl, and tied up my head warmly.

This took us about three minutes, at the end of which time Charlie and Mr Henderson again appeared.

They went to the saloon, where Fanny had played cards a few hours before, and were about to go up on deck when Charlie recalled some things he'd left behind. Telling his mother to wait, he went back to his cabin.

As soon as the ship struck the remainder of the crew came tumbling out of the fo'c'sle. The captain rushed out on deck too.

'Oh dear,' he was heard to say, 'what is the matter? What is the matter?'

The *Strathmore* was tilting over to starboard, water right up to her main-hatch.

Ramsay ordered the men aft. 'All hands clear away the boats!'

Up on the poop, Darkey Fellows was still at the wheel. The sailmaker asked Captain MacDonald if he should fetch sails for the lifeboats, but was told there was no time.

'Clear away the boats, boys,' called the captain. 'Fast as you can.'

Fifteen-year-old apprentice Harold Turner was on the poop.

'Then succeeded a general rush,' he wrote later,

> *some of the passengers getting into the boats before they*
> *were swung out and the sailors pulling them out again; some*
> *swearing, some shouting, some praying; all this, intermingled*
> *with the screams of the women and children and the extreme*
> *darkness of the night, made a scene more easily to be imagined*
> *than described.*
>
> *All was confusion; each one seemed bent on his or her own*
> *safety, and consequently there was much strife.*

Below decks, Charlie was back in his cabin.

> *I unlocked my box, and took out of it a little safe, in which was*
> *£155 in Bank of England notes, enclosed in a sort of leather*
> *pocket-book, and which I put in the breast-pocket of my coat;*
> *also a revolver and a sheath-knife, which afterward turned out*
> *to be invaluable. The latter I put in my belt.*
>
> *The only thing I forgot was a cap; otherwise I was fully*
> *equipped for anything that might turn up.*

Instead of waiting for him, Fanny returned to her own cabin to
fetch her rosary beads and a pair of blankets: 'I ran back to our
cabin … water gurgling and swirling about everywhere.'

She saw Wattie's father, Alfred Walker, 'standing white and
trembling at his cabin door with his child in his arms while his
poor wife was distracted about means of saving the baby'.

When she got back to the saloon, Charlie had not yet
returned. 'Thinking he remained too long, I followed him, and
begged him to come at once, for I heard the captain from the
poop call aloud in an agonised tone, "Now then, come!"'

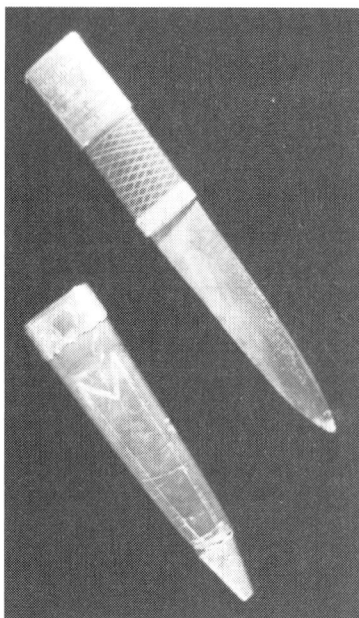

Charlie's invaluable sheath-knife, now in the possession of his grandson Larry Wordsworth

Charlie and Fanny made their way back through the saloon and up to the companion-hatch, which was still partially fastened, leaving only a small hole to pass through. Fanny was forced to drop her load of blankets.

Up on deck, there was a lifeboat and a quarterboat on each side of the ship — the quarterboats being about half the size of the lifeboats. The boats were on skids about two and a half metres off the main deck, close by the poop near the rear of the ship. The quarterboats were stowed in front of the lifeboats, and had to be launched first.

Third mate Allan went over to the port quarterboat with first mate Ramsay and several other men, probably including Black Jack. They hoisted the boat just clear of the chocks on which it rested, then tried to push it out. It would not budge.

'It was so dark,' said Allan later, 'that you could hardly see a person alongside of you.'

They worked on the boat for about five minutes before letting it back down onto the chocks. 'It was jammed, and could not be got out.'

Allan crossed over to help the men working on the starboard quarterboat. 'That was jammed too.'

He returned to the port quarterboat, but found it 'still as tight as ever'. 'You could not shove the quarterboats forward,' he said, 'because of the lifeboats. You could not shove them aft, because of the mizzen rigging.'

Captain MacDonald was standing by the skylight on the poop, talking to the mate: 'I told you it would be so, I told you it would be so.'

Leaving the deck, the captain went down to the saloon to bid his passengers goodbye. Wattie Walker was there with his mother, Alice, in the midst of the noise and confusion.

'It's all lost!' said the captain. 'There is no hope, it's all over! Save yourselves.'

Back on the poop once more, MacDonald paced up and down with his chin on his breast, arms folded.

'He did nothing at all,' said first-class passenger Fred Bentley. 'He seemed heartbroken.'

According to Bentley's cabin-mate, George Crombie, the captain 'seemed incapable of action. He remained walking up and down the poop with his hands behind him, and seemed rather to court his fate.'

Fanny Wordsworth passed the captain on her way to the lifeboats.

'I would have spoken to him,' she wrote later, 'but I knew he was a broken-hearted man.'

She hung onto Charlie's arm as they went over to the starboard lifeboat, followed by the Hendersons. The boat was full of women and children — Mary Riddell, Henrietta Mabille,

Sarah Jane Silk and Betty Goodrich, with little Bertie, Florence and Louisa, and their older brothers and sisters.

As the Wordsworths drew near, Sails bawled out: 'I'll shoot any man who gets in before the women!'

'My mother said she would not get into the first boat,' wrote Charlie later, 'as very likely I should be separated from her.'

'If there is not room for you,' said Fanny, 'there is not for me.'

They went on until they came to the other boats. 'Just then,' wrote Fanny,

> I heard Mrs Walker, who unfortunately had got separated from her husband and child, ask Charlie to look for him, but he did not hear her; he was considering how I could be got into the port lifeboat.
>
> 'Can you get on the bridge, Mother?' he asked.
>
> I said 'Yes' — though it was a place I dared not have attempted in daylight on a calm day.
>
> I got into it, I know not how. Charlie and a sailor named Jack … pulled me up into the boat by the hands.
>
> The moment I was lifted from the quarter-deck a sea swept over it, some of the water splashing on my face. That sea washed Miss Henderson from her brother's arms down to the main deck, and so the poor child was lost.

Probably this wave swept Wattie's mother away too, along with a number of the men who'd been trying to launch the boats.

In Charlie's opinion, 'the only chance of safety lay in getting into the lifeboat, cutting the gripes, and trusting to Providence that when the ship went down, as I then supposed her to be doing, the lifeboat would float off clear of the wreck'.

'By this time,' wrote second mate Thomas Brown Peters in his account of the wreck, 'the seas came rolling over the poop in quick succession, making it impossible for us to get [the] boat[s] out and scattering the men who were working with me, a good many of them being washed overboard and drowned … As the ship was now fast settling down aft, the most of those who had been working at the quarterboats now got into the port lifeboat …'

Fanny and Charlie sat waiting in the lifeboat.

'A few farewells were exchanged,' wrote Fanny. 'I said goodbye to my dear boy, and a pang of anguish went through me for his young life, so soon to be taken.'

Wattie and his father were still on deck, and so was second mate Peters.

> I found Mr Walker (saloon passenger) standing, holding on to the poop rail with [his] little boy in his arms, not knowing what to do. I took it [Wattie] from him and carried it up the mizzen rigging, where I passed it to the second steward, afterwards coming down again to see if I could help any other unfortunates …

Young Farmer John was already aloft when Peters climbed up with Wattie: 'I had picked up a life-buoy, which I had taken up in the rigging with me where I had taken refuge. I was not to have it long, for as I sat in the mizen top, the second mate ordered me to give it to a passenger and his baby, saying it was better that two should be saved than one. I at once gave it to him.'

By now there were nine sailors and nine passengers huddled together in the port lifeboat. Fanny was the only woman among them.

> … we were preparing ourselves as well as we could to meet our God, when, wonderful to relate, a heavy sea came sweeping along over the poop, carrying everything with it to destruction; but instead of dashing our boat to pieces, or tumbling it from

the beams on which it stood down to the deck, it caught it up and miraculously floated us between the main and mizzen rigging into the sea.

I thought at the time we were going quietly into eternity.

The wave 'washed us clean over the starboard side,' wrote Charlie, 'knocking down on its way a strong rail, the "standard compass," &c., and [our boat] reached the sea in safety, though a little "stove in". The wonder was the sea did not take us down into the main deck, for the waves were running almost in a straight line from aft, forward.'

'I felt Charlie's grasp tighten,' wrote Fanny, 'and with a prayer on my lips I think I almost was gone.'

The teenaged Joslen boys — surveyor Percy and his younger brother, Spencer — saw the port lifeboat as she floated for a moment in the eddy on the starboard side.

'Both immediately made for it,' said seventeen-year-old Spencer later. He 'managed to reach the weather rigging safely, and thence swing ... into the lifeboat ... but another sea came over the poop', and Percy was drowned.

'We had hardly breathed,' wrote Fanny, 'when Charlie suddenly almost threw me from him, and wrenching an oar out, shouted, "Saved! saved! by a miracle. Up, lads, and keep her off the ship!"'

As it came rolling over the poop to free the lifeboat, the wave also carried away Captain MacDonald, first mate Ramsay and helmsman Darkey Fellows, Darkey still clutching part of the wheel in his hand. All three men drowned.

Just as the port lifeboat was floated clear, the port quarterboat was smashed to pieces and both starboard boats were washed off their chocks and lost overboard. The starboard lifeboat capsized, drowning everyone in it:

- Newly wed farmer and second-class passenger James Riddell
- His wife, Mary, who'd waited eight years for him
- 39-year-old civil engineer and second-class passenger Theophilus Mabille
- His wife, Henrietta, ten years younger — in Fanny's words, 'a merry laughing creature'
- 27-year-old saleswoman and steerage passenger Sarah Jane Silk
- Her younger brother, Frank, a land surveyor
- Agriculturalist and steerage passenger Edward Goodrich
- His wife, Elizabeth
- Their eight children — Frederick, eighteen; Elizabeth, fourteen; Rebecca, eleven; Hester Jane, nine; Edward, six; Bertie, five; Florence, two; Louisa, one
- Around half a dozen single men, mostly steerage passengers, their names now lost

Many of them could not swim and some were in heavy clothes which dragged them down. Those who did not drown immediately had nowhere to swim for — they were tossed about in the water, clutching onto debris in the darkness. Some were killed by waves dashing them against rocks and others passed out from the cold — it did not take long in those waters.

'There were no screams or cries,' said one of the third-class passengers who'd made it into the rigging. 'It was pitch dark.'

A miserable time of it till daylight

By the time the lifeboats were swept into the sea — about fifteen minutes after the ship hit the rocks — the deck of the *Strathmore* was tilting down toward her stern. The prow of the ship jutted up out of the waves, while her poop was completely underwater. Waves broke over the vessel, crashing and fizzing around the masts and deckhouses.

Though she had not capsized, the port lifeboat was perilously close to the ship.

'The boat,' wrote Charlie, 'when it reached the sea, was still foul of the main brace, and as we thought the ship was going down every moment, we made strenuous efforts to get clear.'

While the men worked at the oars, Fanny sat shivering in the dark,

> ... trying to comfort and warm poor Spencer Joslen, who had hurt himself jumping into the boat ...
>
> It was pitch dark, in the dead of a winter night. We had few clothes, and the boat having been stove in on its passage across the deck, we were sitting almost up to our waists in water. Huge sprays washed over our shoulders; and so, surrounded by breakers and sharp rocks, we did not know which way to turn for safety ...
>
> By dint of hard labour, and great caution, we managed to keep clear of every obstacle ... Indeed, had she not been a splendid lifeboat we should very soon have sunk.
>
> We beat about all night, not knowing where we went, afraid of being drifted out to sea without food or water. Breakers ahead! and Land, ho! was the cry all night.

'Half of us were engaged in baling,' wrote Charlie,

> ... but we might have saved ourselves the trouble, for the water neither decreased nor increased, the air-tight tanks keeping her afloat. The rest that were able pulled at the oars.

It was this night I lost my £155. I had taken my coat off to pull an oar, and it was then I think I lost it; for most likely it dropped out of my pocket and was baled overboard during the night, for I never saw it again, and the list of the numbers of the notes I had left on board.

We spent a miserable time of it till daylight, dodging about in the darkness and fog, trying to keep clear of the rocks, breakers, and large quantities of sea-weed, and yet keep near land.

While the lifeboat was lurching and tossing about in the surf, most of those left on board the wreck clung to the sodden rigging, numb and shivering in their wet clothes. The ship's masts shuddered and groaned with the pounding of the sea, and the loose canvas of the sails thwacked and billowed in the icy wind.

There is no record of Black Jack's whereabouts during these hours. He may have been in the lifeboat with Fanny and Charlie, but most likely he'd fled to the mizzentop by the time the boats were washed from the ship. The mizzentop is a small wooden platform, one-third of the way up the mizzenmast — the hindmost mast on a three-master like the *Strathmore*.

'The top was crowded,' said one third-class passenger. There were between ten and twenty sailors and passengers there, huddled together in the rain and wind.

Believing the ship was going down stern first, second mate Peters told the men they had 'better go down the fore and aft stays and try and get forward'.

If he was on the mizzentop, Black Jack would have been among those who climbed up to the cross-trees (two-thirds of the way up the mast) to reach the mizzen topmast stay, a rope stretching across to the mainmast. Elbows and knees hooked over the damp, swaying rope, the men inched across through the dark. Some of them did not make it beyond the mainmast that night.

'A little Scotch boy and I came down the mizen stay,' wrote apprentice Harold Turner, probably referring to the sixteen-year-old ordinary seaman John Leask, known as 'Young Jock',

> and on arriving at the bottom we could proceed no further, we were so completely benumbed with the cold. The seas and pieces of wreck kept constantly washing over us. The Scotch boy let go ... being quite unable to hold on any longer ... He was just being washed overboard when, by accident, he caught hold of the main topsail halyards, and so was able to get on the shrouds and ascend with very great difficulty into the maintop.
>
> All this time, I was ... making efforts to climb a little higher. Being so very cold and benumbed, I was quite an hour in going the distance I could otherwise have gone in a minute or two.
>
> One of the sailors, on getting to the bottom of the stay, dropped off, and ... ran along the deck a little way, when suddenly there came a tremendous wave and washed him overboard.

This was able seaman Philip Cogan, one of Black Jack's watch-mates.

From the mainmast, the rest of the men climbed along the mainstay to the roof of the forward deckhouse, where the ship's gig and dinghy were lashed.

'When we reached the top of the house,' said second mate Peters, 'we found a few of the crew and passengers already there, so we turned the gig upon her keel ready for launching at daybreak, as it was too dark then for us to risk our last chance of getting clear of the ship.'

After preparing the boats for launching they made them fast. 'Then we went on to the forecastle-head,' said third mate Allan, 'where we stopped till day broke.'

Among those left behind on the mizzentop was little Wattie. Hour after hour he clung to his father in the freezing Antarctic southwester, his nightclothes wet through in the thick fog and drizzling rain. The mast shook and buckled as the waves battered the *Strathmore*, and the men readied themselves to swim ashore in case their precarious shelter gave way.

The four or five hours before dawn would have seemed a long time to the adult survivors, but how much longer for Wattie? Two-and-a-half years old, freezing cold, soaking wet, terrified and disoriented in the roaring black of the night — those first four hours of life without his mother must have stretched into forever.

High perpendicular rock

By the time dawn finally came, around half past eight on the bitterly cold morning of Thursday, 1 July, the *Strathmore* was underwater except for her forward deckhouse, fo'c'sle-head and upper masts. Screaming seabirds wheeled overhead, and the seas around the vessel were littered with bobbing cargo and wreckage.

Now that it was light, though still foggy, Peters and the other men on the fo'c'sle-head could see that the bow of the ship 'was jammed between two rocks, and … there was no immediate danger'.

Not everyone was safe, however.

'At daylight,' Peters said, 'a third-class passenger, who had been a soldier [probably the forty-year-old pensioner Peter Hurford], was hanging [on] to the mizzen-mast when a sea came and washed him away.'

The wreck of the Strathmore, *from a sketch by ship's carpenter John Pirie*

Meanwhile, because of the fog and the size of the swell, the survivors in the lifeboat could see little beyond the nearest wave.

'We were very nearly losing land altogether,' wrote Charlie. 'We had just made up our minds to run off before the wind and give all our energies to baling out the boat when the fog lifted, and we saw the big rocks looming out ...'

Between two waves, the shivering survivors caught a glimpse of the ship. 'She was leaning over a good deal,' wrote Fanny, 'and looked very helpless and forlorn, and so sad.'

Up on the fo'c'sle-head, Black Jack and the other men now had a clear view of Grande Île, the largest landmass in the Twelve Apostles, the northernmost islands of the Crozet Archipelago. It was a sobering sight.

One first-class passenger saw rocks 'about 100 yards [away], rising off like a wall several hundreds of feet out of the water'. The second mate disputed the distance — 'the ship was within about thirty yards from a perpendicular cliff' — though he agreed the cliff was 'hundreds of feet high', and added that there were 'other rocks all round about the ship, some of them being awash and others standing up sharp, like so many needles'.

Fifteen-year-old Harold Turner saw the rocks this way.

> *As the day began to unfold, we were gradually able to perceive a large rock in the shape of a sugar-loaf, about two masts high, towering far above our heads. We were so close, that the bowsprit nearly touched it … The cliffs were about two thousand feet high; but, being covered with the clouds, we were unable to see the summit.*
>
> *None can possibly picture the scene but those who saw it. There was our beautiful ship, which a few hours before was gaily riding the glass-like ocean; but now, alas! all that was left was a scanty wreck, with a few human creatures clinging to it for their life. On the one side was the cruel, merciless sea, and on the other stupendous rocks and cliffs.*

'Taking it all together,' said the second mate, 'it made us launch the remaining two boats that we might find better quarters, if they were to be found.'

The sea was level with the roof of the deckhouse by now, and 'breaking still higher at times, there being a heavy surf running'.

According to third-class passenger Robert Aitkenhead Wilson (who was linked to the ship's officers through his brother, second steward David Wilson, and who did secretarial work for the captain), Peters had trouble with some of the sailors: 'The second mate called to the crew on the forecastle head to come and launch the gig and dinghy, [but] the greater part of them would not obey, so we went to the deckhouse and launched the boats.'

Young Harold Turner must have been one of the few obedient crew members. 'The lashings which held the gig and dinghy we cut,' he said, 'and, after some little trouble we got them right side up and launched.'

During embarkation, the bottom of the dinghy was damaged. As Peters explained, the leak was lessened by leaving the canvas cover on the boat, so that she was 'able to carry three with tolerable safety'.

He went on board the gig with one of the passengers. 'They got her under the lee foreyard,' said Aitkenhead Wilson. 'There was then a scramble for the rigging, and we got into the braces and from there into the boat.'

Four men got into the dinghy, and about eight into the gig, including Peters, Aitkenhead Wilson, Hilton Keith from first class, the young sailor Charles Tookey, the sailmaker and Black Jack.

'I'll be back again,' Peters called to the men left behind on the ship. 'If not, I hope we shall be better off.'

They rowed the gig eastwards, along the northern end of the island. Waves slapped against the sides of the boat. The men braced their feet on the planks and threw their weight into their stroke, growing a little warmer despite the sharp wind and showers of icy spray. Unable to find a landing place, they continued some three kilometres around the south side. Eventually Peters found a place where the terraces rose more gradually from the sea, and they could 'scramble ashore, although with great danger to the boat'. But before they reached the landing place, they were hailed by the port lifeboat.

'I was the first to see another boat,' wrote Fanny. 'I gave a joyful scream, and the second mate, Mr Peters, with some passengers and sailors, came to us and towed us to land.'

Towing the almost swamped lifeboat caused what Peters called 'a good deal of trouble'. There was a heavy swell, a strong north-east current, and masses of snaking seaweed, and the oarsmen were tired and hungry. Things didn't get any easier when they finally reached the landing place, which was, explained Charlie, 'a ledge on the face of the perpendicular rock … to reach which a man had to watch his chance when the swell took the boat up, catch hold of parts of the rock, and haul himself up a height of about twelve feet from the sea'.

'I gave up in despair,' wrote Fanny,

> for I saw nothing but a high perpendicular rock before me, impossible almost for a goat to find footing on …
>
> I am not very clever at climbing at the best of times, but weak and ill, stiff with cold, and dripping wet, I felt I had no life in me, and could not do it.
>
> I said, 'Charlie, I can't do it; you must leave me.'
>
> 'Nonsense,' he said; and one of the seamen, Jack Wilson, added, 'If there is anybody to be saved you will be.'
>
> The sailors who had already mounted the rock soon managed to lower a rope with a loop in it, in which I sat, and was pulled up, assisted by Charlie and young Mr Keith on either side.

'My mother was hoisted up in a "bowline",' wrote Charlie, 'a knot she now firmly believes in.'

Once Fanny was safely landed — the only woman out of the seven on board the *Strathmore* to make it ashore — the men from the lifeboat pulled themselves up the rock using the boat's painter, followed by the four passengers from the gig.

As soon as they were on land, the hungry men began hunting for seabirds. Cornering the birds among the rocks, they kicked them to death, clubbed them with stones or simply grabbed them and wrung their necks.

'I was stunned with cold,' wrote Fanny,

and almost fainting, so that it seemed only a few minutes to me
till Charlie came with the reeking-hot skins of two albatrosses
and wrapped my feet in them. Oh, how delightful it was!

Someone knocked down a white pigeon, which was cooked
on some sticks and given to me. I thought I had never tasted
anything so good.

While Fanny was eating pigeon, the men on the fo'c'sle-head
waited anxiously for Peters' return. Cold and hungry, they were
huddled on the wet decking with nowhere to hide from the rain
and wind and spray, surrounded by the constant roaring of the
sea.

'It was indeed a day,' wrote the young apprentice Harold
Turner, 'one ever to be remembered. It seemed more like a
week than a few hours; suspense and hunger … were very hard
to endure.'

At the far end of the ship from Harold, Wattie Walker
crouched close to the warmth of his father on the slanting
mizzentop. Aside from the three steerage passengers who'd not
attempted to climb forward along the stays, they were the only
ones left in the after part of the ship. The men on the fo'c'sle-
head did not even know they were there.

The boards of the mizzentop were sodden and slippery,
shuddering and swaying in the icy wind. Wattie's small body was
soaking wet and shivering, his belly empty, his mother gone.

Back at the landing place, the four men still in the gig —
Peters, Black Jack, Sails and another — were preparing to return
to the wreck. Someone threw the painter back into the boat, and
the men on board shoved off hard. They dropped down into their
seats, seized the oars and rowed as fast as they could through the
snarls of seaweed, sprinting to keep from being slammed back
into the rock. Safely away from the cliff they settled down to a

steady rhythm, perhaps singing a shanty to keep time, if they had breath to spare.

On their way back to the wreck they met the dinghy, which had gotten lost in the swell. Peters told the third mate where to find the landing place, and the two boats passed each other, one heading to the island, the other to the ship.

Nearing the wreck, they hailed their shipmates on the fo'c'sle-head, then rowed past them to the survivors in the mizzentop — Peters judging that 'they were in greater danger there'.

The surf was running too high for the gig to come right up to the ship, so Peters called out to the survivors to climb out from the mizzentop onto the crossjack yardarm — the outer end of the wooden spar slung across the mizzenmast for the lowermost sail to hang from. Mr Walker and his boy, he said, must go first.

Somehow Alfred and Wattie got off the mizzentop and onto the yard, hung for an instant above the churning waves, and let go. Free-falling, they plunged under the icy water, rose to the surface, and were hauled struggling and spluttering onto the boat. One by one the men from steerage followed — climbing onto the yard and dropping into the sea to be picked up.

'After a good deal of danger,' said Peters, 'we got all there were in the mizzentop aboard the boat ... As the night was fast closing in ... I sung out to those left on the forecastle-head to cheer up, as I would come back for them first thing in the morning ...'

'They went off,' said one of the men left behind, 'and we were left shivering in the cold ...'

Landed

By the time the gig again reached the island, the light was beginning to fade. The sailors on shore had roped the empty lifeboat and dinghy to a rock. Both boats were leaking badly, and were described by Peters as '... little better than useless ... certainly not safe to venture back to the ship in'. The twenty-nine survivors already landed — sixteen sailors, a dozen male passengers and Fanny — had moved uphill to a rock ledge about ten metres above the landing place, where, Charlie wrote, they 'sat huddled together ... wet, cold, hungry, and miserable'.

They had lit a fire using wood from the wreck, on which they were roasting young albatrosses and other 'sea-fowl'. The birds were repulsive — rank, fishy and half-raw. Some of the survivors could not stomach the flesh at all, hungry as they were. There was nothing else to sustain them except a small ration of alcohol — the sailors in the gig had picked up a few cases of spirits on their way back from the wreck.

When the gig arrived, the men took its canvas cover and stretched it and the dinghy cover over some oars to make a shelter, which, according to Charlie, 'came down during the night and made matters worse'. It was not nearly big enough for thirty-eight people, but both Fanny and Wattie were given places inside.

'We put in a miserable night,' wrote Peters later, 'the softest rock being our bed, which was not rendered more agreeable by the coldness of the weather.'

According to third-class passenger Robert Aitkenhead Wilson, the second mate had a particularly unsettled sleep, 'lying half under the tent and calling out all night giving orders as if he were on board'.

It was a bad night for all the survivors, in or out of the flimsy, overcrowded shelter. Hungry, wet, freezing cold and almost impossibly uncomfortable on their hard beds, most of them were probably in shock. Charlie remembered it this way:

The first night ashore was dreadful; we lay exposed on the rocks, huddled together for warmth, the rain pouring down and chilling us to the marrow … My mother, in consideration of her sex, had some planks to lie upon, but she was wofully [sic] crushed, and her legs nearly broken, by people crowding in under the canvas. Though greatly fatigued, few of us slept …

None of the survivors' accounts mention Wattie crying during the night — perhaps he was so exhausted that he slept, despite the hard rock and the cold, or perhaps he was too bewildered to make a noise.

Fanny had lost her shawl, which had been used to try to stop the leak in the lifeboat.

It was so cold I was nearly frozen to death.

Some of the sailors, for whose kindness I can never be sufficiently grateful … covered me with their coats, but they were taken from me during the night by some of the passengers, and then, Oh the agony I suffered in my limbs! Mr Keith and Charlie had to move my feet and hands, and when I could bear it no longer I went outside and sat by a small fire they had lit.

Black Jack gave me his own stockings … which were warm, for I had none — the crew were all so kind to me.

Eighteen-year-old Robert Aitkenhead Wilson, who had strong religious opinions, was less favourably impressed by the seamen: 'There was a fire outside the tent … some of the sailors got around it and would not move. Some of them appeared to be drunk.'

Black Jack, very likely, was among the possibly drunken sailors, pressed up close to his mates for warmth, no stockings

Robert Aitkenhead Wilson, third-class passenger, who passed a miserable first night on Grande Île

under his trousers. The men were surrounded by darkness, and by the roar of the sea, much louder than they were used to on board ship, as it crashed into the base of the cliffs below them. The fire smoked and sputtered, sheltered a little by the overhanging rock, and perhaps helped along with salvaged gunpowder — how else could they keep it alight in the rain and wind, with waterlogged wood? Huddled together in their wet clothes, the sailors stared into the flickering flames and warmed themselves with rum. They made room for Fanny when she got up, but not for young Aitkenhead Wilson. He was outside on the bare rock until around six on Friday morning, when Peters and others got up to launch the boats, leaving room for Wilson to get under the canvas.

Another third-class passenger, 26-year-old George Mellor, an engineer from Huddersfield, had been acting strangely during the night. He seemed dazed and tried to jump head-first into the fire. In the early morning some men carried Mellor into the tent and laid him right on top of the sleeping Aitkenhead Wilson.

'He died before I got up,' said Wilson, 'but I was not aware of it till he was moved off.'

The cause of Mellor's death was reported variously as shock, cold, exhaustion, fright and exposure. According to the apprentice Harold Turner, who was not there, two men threw Mellor's body 'over the cliff, as they could not very conveniently bury him, being afraid lest Mrs Wordsworth might see the corpse'.

On board the *Strathmore*, in one passenger's words, the night had passed 'in misery and terror ...' The sea washed continually over the wreck, coming right up to the break of the fo'c'sle. 'What with the spray which saturated our clothing,' wrote Harold Turner, 'and the cold, we were almost frozen lifeless. The misery of the awful suspense, and the horrid fancies and dreams, were almost unbearable ...'

Eventually the men managed to light a fire on the fo'c'sle-head, using some wreckage and saved matches — probably it saved their lives.

Daylight once more dawned, and what that day would bring forth we knew not. Our great fear was that the vessel would not hold together. There were no signs of the boats, but plenty of wreckage floating about to remind us of our unpleasant condition ...

About ten o'clock, we were thinking of making a raft and going in search of the boats. We were afraid the gig and her crew must have been lost. We were looking in the direction in which she went the previous night, when one of us happened to turn round, and there, to our great surprise, she was close upon us. We gave three hearty cheers.

The sea was smoother than it had been the day before, and the oarsmen were able to get the boat near the wreck.

'I made the men that were on the forecastle-head get all the clothes they could out of the forecastle,' wrote Peters later,

> and pass them into the boat before I took them aboard themselves, the most of them that were ashore being only half-clad ... The poop, deckhouse and forecastle being completely gutted, I could get neither provisions, cooking utensils, nor useful implements of any kind, the only things we did get being a few sticks of tobacco, one dozen biscuits and a small meat cleaver.

We were not long in ascending the foreyard and forebrace into the boat,' wrote Harold Turner.

> When we were about one hundred yards from the vessel, we had one more look at our old home. It was, indeed, a pitiful sight. There she was on her beam-ends, all her stern under water, and her lee rigging swinging loosely about. A heavy swell rolled loosely over her, and death-like noises came from her inside.

Some of those rescued from the fo'c'sle-head were so weak they had to lie down in the boat on the way back to the island.

'On landing,' wrote Peters, 'we gave the biscuits to Mrs Wordsworth, as the birds' flesh was so rank that she could not eat it.' Perhaps the 'pigeon' (or Crozet Island sheathbill) that Fanny had eaten on arrival was more tender and more scarce than the albatross.

As well as biscuits, Harold Turner records that Fanny was given 'a pair of trousers, some taking off their shirts and jackets, to protect her from the severe cold'. She remembers it this way:

> Walter Smith, the sailmaker, and Mike O'Riordan, an A.B., brought me a suit of manly garments — Mike giving me the

*shirt from his back. Trousers, my flannel petticoat, and a
'monkey jacket' completed my outfit; but either the trousers were
curiously made or else I was, for we did not get on well together.*

According to Harold, the passengers were less generous than
the sailors.

*I never met with a more selfish set of men than most of the
passengers were, they took care to look after number one. As soon
as the clothing came ashore, the passengers put it on, some taking
two or three shirts, two pairs of trousers, besides drawers and
jackets, whilst some of the poor sailors were nearly half naked.*

There is no record of anyone giving Wattie extra clothing,
although, according to a third-class passenger, 'Everything that
was any use was given to … [Mrs Wordsworth] and to the child.'
Perhaps Wattie was given some ship's biscuits, as he too had trouble
eating the seabirds. Also known as hardtack or tooth dullers, ship's
biscuits were baked four times to prevent spoilage on long voyages,
which made them notoriously hard — very different to the soft
sago and rice Wattie had been used to eating on board ship.

The wreck had changed almost every detail of his life.

Throughout the rest of Friday, 2 July, the boats went to and fro,
from landing place to ship, carrying back whatever they could
salvage. Though the swell was not as big as the day before, the
waves were plenty high enough for the little boats. Freezing
winds whipped spray into the faces of the rowers. They used
all three boats, though the lifeboat and dinghy had been judged
unfit to return to the wreck the day before. Perhaps the sailors
had managed to repair them, or maybe it was easier to keep
them afloat in the calmer seas.

On one of their journeys, the men saw the starboard lifeboat
— the boat that had carried the Goodrich children and the
women from second and third class. It was floating bottom
upwards near the wreck.

Second mate Peters directed the salvaging effort, and, as Fanny
wrote, 'was ably assisted by some of the men, among whom were
Walter Smith, sailmaker, and "Black Jack". These two I noticed
particularly, they being the only sailors I knew the names of.'

The second mate was hoping to retrieve the ship's sails, to
use for making shelters, but the surf was so high about the
wreck that they couldn't get back on board: '… we had to be
content to pick up what we could find floating around her,
such as firewood, a few cases of spirits, a cask of wine, a case
of confectionery [jam] … and a few other articles which we
thought would be useful'.

According to Fanny, Peters refused to let Charlie on the boats,
'saying his duty was to take care of me'.

Instead, Charlie helped to explore the island, scrambling up
and down the cliffs and gullies in the wind, sea roaring all around,
seabirds screaming overhead: '… we found it to be about two
and a half kilometres long, and a good part of that was rock and
stones, the rest being covered with a long, coarse grass. There
was no firewood … but we had lots of splendid water.'

One of the third-class passengers estimated the island to be
nearer three kilometres long and about 500 metres across in the
widest place. There was a comparatively low central plateau,
climbing to about 175 metres at the western end (less than one-
third of Harold Turner's 2000 feet) and 125 metres at the eastern
end, with steep cliffs dropping into the sea from each summit.
Most of the shoreline was impossible to approach by boat
and the only beach was a narrow line of sand hidden beneath
overhanging cliffs near the wreck. On such a small island there

was not much to discover. 'There were no signs of anybody having been on the island before,' said the third mate.

They did find an overhanging rock about halfway up the cliff, and the men on shore spent much of the rest of Friday constructing a wall of stones on a ledge beneath the overhang. They built the wall about two and a half metres away from the cliff, binding the stones together with turf and mud. It was not an easy job. Buffeted by the freezing winds, they dug the rocks out of the guano with their bare hands.

'The cold was so great,' said saloon passenger George Crombie, 'as to render touching the stones a very painful work.'

Young Harold Turner may have been thinking of Crombie when he recalled an 'amusing incident' that occurred during the day.

> One of the saloon passengers had been out in search of whatever he might find. In his travels, he killed an albatross, and upon returning, he commenced to eat one of its legs.
>
> 'Steward,' said he to that worthy, who was standing by, 'have you got a knife and fork anywhere?'
>
> It seemed so ridiculous to us all to ask for such a thing there, that we could not help having a hearty good laugh.

Apparently the men were not superstitious about killing albatrosses. Notable instances of seamen eating albatrosses include those recorded in Captain Cook's journals — the idea that sailors believed it unlucky to harm the birds seems to owe more to Coleridge's poem *The Rime of the Ancient Mariner* than to historical fact.

At dusk the sailors returned from salvaging. They roped the boats together and looped the end of the painter over a projecting rock on the sheltered side of the island — the cliffs were too steep to pull the boats up on shore. By the time they got back to the camp they found a wall about six metres long, but less than a metre high. They got the canvas boat covers and a couple of salvaged sheets, stretched them down from the rock overhang toward the half-built wall, and anchored them at top and bottom with heavy boulders and wire stays. There was still a sizable gap to let the weather in. 'It was blowing a gale,' noted one of the passengers.

After eating a supper of half-cooked albatross, the survivors made a plan for the following day. Some of the men would continue gathering cargo and wreckage in the gig and dinghy, while others would row the lifeboat across to explore the large island they had seen to the south-west: Hog Island, about twenty kilometres away, where perhaps they would find sealers' huts, wild pigs and firewood.

They sang a few hymns before settling down for the night. 'As there was a Bible saved from the wreck,' wrote Peters in his diary, 'we held a sort of service ... both to pray for a speedy rescue from this miserable island and to thank God for our deliverance ...'

The half-built hut gave better shelter than the previous night's tent, but there was no way all forty-eight survivors could cram into the three- by six-metre space between the cliff-face and the wall.

'As we cannot all sleep under one ledge,' wrote Peters, 'some of us had to find other holes in the rock, where we could stow ourselves away ...'

Even so, it was an almost impossibly tight fit — 'the place was so small that we could only sit huddled together as close as we could possibly pack.'

Wattie Walker and his father squeezed into the hut, but Fanny and Charlie could not face a second night of extreme overcrowding: '... my mother and myself, with one or two others, slept in a sort of open cave, or rather overhanging ledge of rock, a little higher up than we were before; and though the frost lay on our blankets, and the icicles over our heads, yet it was pleasant to what the other place had been.'

Black Jack avoided the crush in the hut by going down to the water's edge with Yankee Bill Vining, to keep watch over the boats. They sat in the lee of a rock near the place where the painter was made fast, their knees drawn up to their chins against the icy cold.

Lashed together at the far end of the rope, the three boats formed one dark shape in the dusk, bobbing up and down on the swell. Night came down, and the gale grew stronger.

Utterly stranded

It was a wild night. Gale-force winds lashed the island, whipping the sea into a high, chaotic surf. Some time during that Friday evening, or early on the Saturday morning, the gig, dinghy and lifeboat came away from their moorings.

'The wind chopping suddenly broke them adrift,' said the second mate, 'and we had the pleasure of seeing them floating about bottom up, completely out of our reach.'

Without boats the survivors were utterly stranded, with no hope of making their way to a more hospitable island, or of salvaging anything more from the wreck. They were stuck on tiny Grande Île — despite its name, a bleak, treeless rock in the middle of the ocean.

They were short of clothing and had no proper shelter. Their food was all but inedible, and there was no source of firewood beyond the little they had already gathered from the ship. 'We thought then,' wrote Harold Turner, 'that our only chance for life had gone.'

In their distress, some of the men asked themselves whether they had done enough to prevent their loss.

'I sent down three of the best of the crew to watch the boats,' lamented the second mate in his diary, 'which were moored in smooth water … it being impossible to draw them up on shore … If there had been a beach anywhere on the island we might have saved them by hauling them up, but the island was so steep and rugged that we could scarcely scramble ashore ourselves, much less haul boats ashore.'

Charlie wondered whether they should have manned the boats, instead of merely keeping watch over them from the land: '… some might think the boats could have been saved by people keeping in them'.

But he defended the survivors from the imputation of negligence: '… how could any of us manage to keep them safe, broken up and leaky as the boats were, even if we had gone to the lee side of the island and kept pulling in shore against a terrible gale for two or three days, exhausted for want of food, wet, and most likely frozen? It could not have been kept up for two hours.'

Others implied the loss was connected with the lookout men. 'While Black Jack and William Vining were in charge of the boats that night,' said Robert Aitkenhead Wilson, 'they were lost.'

Although first-class passenger Spencer Joslen did not mention names, he was more explicit as to the possible cause of the loss, stating that 'three of the crew were drunk the night after the wreck. One of them was employed to look after the boats.'

Able seaman John Wilson was also clear as to where the blame lay: 'The boats were lost owing to the drunkenness of the two men in charge.'

Others disagreed with them. 'We found the men in charge drunk next morning,' said the third mate, 'but had they been sober, the sea was running so high that I do not think they could have kept the boats.'

The second mate maintained that Black Jack and Yankee Bill had not been drunk while on duty. They'd reported the loss of the boats to him at daybreak, being unable, in the dark, to climb up the rocks to the camp. Peters was 'asleep at the time and not in a fit condition to notice whether they were then drunk or not, but thought they were not'.

When he came down the hill a little later in the morning he found the men drunk beside a thirty-gallon wine cask. The cask was three-quarters full, lying 'bung down, and would have lost more if they had got at it long before'. In any case, according to Peters, the loss of the boats would have been 'impossible to prevent, on account of the high surf running'.

Exactly what happened is unclear. Were two or three men assigned to lookout duty? Did two or three men get drunk? Were one, two or three of the drunk men on lookout? Did the men get drunk the night before or the morning after? Could sober men have saved the boats?

And how did the survivors react, faced with such enormous disappointment? Was Black Jack openly blamed? Did he deny the charge or admit responsibility?

No matter who did what, or what anyone thought, the three boats were gone — 'lost to us forever', wrote Fanny, 'a great calamity'.

'We saw the boats afterwards,' added Charlie, 'on the other side of the island still attached to each other by their painters, but smashed and bottom up, they having been driven by the gale through a tunnel that ran underneath the island, and caught for a time in some sea-weed …'

According to Peters the lifeboat was in halves, the gig and dinghy capsized. The cliff was too steep for the men to climb down to them. 'The rocks there were precipitous, 200 feet high, and though attempts were made to get down and recover the boats it was found to be impossible.'

During the storm in which the boats were lost, the *Strathmore* had sunk entirely beneath the waves, along with all her valuable cargo, sails, rope and other equipment, as well as a great deal of firewood. A hunting party which went over to the north side of the island on the Saturday morning saw the ship, and told the second mate that she had 'backed astern and gone down in deep water ...'

This was an additional blow, as the survivors had hoped they could board the wreck again, even without boats, by getting down the cliffs and swimming out to her.

'During the day,' wrote Peters, 'some of us walked over the island to have a look at the wreck, but nothing was to be seen of her but a few small spars entangled by some of the gear and so kept floating over the site of the wreck ... I had intended to get some gear out of her to build a house with, and some ropes, and if possible some cooking utensils ...'

Several days later the men tried to get down to the wreck site anyway, on the chance they could gather some floating wreckage, but 'found it to be impossible to get down to her from the cliff without rope'.

On Wednesday, 7 July, four days after the loss of the boats, Peters recorded that:

> ... there was a possibility of getting the boats with the help of a few oars lashed together; so, after swallowing our breakfast, we climbed over to the other side of the island, close to where our boats were lying in a lot of seaweed; but it was impossible to do anything, for we could find no way of getting to the water's edge.

Before we came away we had the mortification to see our boats float away to sea, dinghy and gig being fast together, and the lifeboat by itself ...

We don't know whether Wattie was standing by the men as they watched the upturned boats drifting toward the horizon, or, if he was, whether he understood what was happening. But surely he sensed the grown-ups' feelings.

4

Exile

Like most days in the Crozet Islands, Saturday, 3 July 1875, was blustery and bitterly cold. Toward evening, the *Strathmore* survivors gathered for what one passenger called 'a council of ways and means'. They huddled close together to try and keep warm, speaking loudly over the crashing of the waves.

Much had happened in the last three days. They had lost their ship — their only home for the preceding two and a half months — along with almost everything they owned. Over forty of their shipmates had died. And now their three small boats were gone, destroying their only immediate hope of getting off the tiny barren rock on which they were stranded.

'You never saw such an uncompromising place,' wrote Fanny.

Still reeling from the shipwreck, and filled with what Charlie called 'the dread of being compelled to stop long on the island', they now had to find food, fuel and shelter to keep themselves alive for the next days, weeks, maybe months or even years.

Almost nine months after that blustery Saturday, on 29 March 1876, a London *Times* editorial on the *Strathmore* wreck reflected on the predicament of the castaway: 'The notion of being cast on a desert island … has something in it not altogether displeasing to the fancy,' mused the *Times* journalist.

The adventures of Robinson Crusoe have entered so deeply into our minds, and have formed so large and so delightful a part of our literary experiences, that the grown man bears still the impress which the boy received, and though he would not, perhaps, willingly share the fate of his old favourite, yet it would be without any great sense of dismay that he would find himself forced to do so.

But one or two circumstances must be granted to make such a lot tolerable. The ship from which Crusoe was saved broke up gradually, and he had ... abundant opportunities of supplying himself with a great many things of which he was ... in want. The island, too, on which Crusoe was cast was ... far from unfit to be the dwelling-place of man.

Grande Île, however, as one first-class passenger said later, is 'a desolate place, a refuge of seabirds, and devoid of trees'.

The weather in the Crozets is cold, wet and constantly windy. Snow, sleet, hail and ice are common. Winds often exceed one

Grande Île, as painted by Charlie

hundred kilometres an hour, and it rains three hundred days a
year.

And the *Strathmore*, unlike Crusoe's ship, sank within forty-
eight hours, severely limiting the opportunities for salvage. 'I
think,' wrote Fanny,

> ... *the following articles were all that were saved. Some tins
> of Keiller's jams — Bless him for making them so strong, for
> afterwards they were all that we had to cook in — some cases
> of spirits and a cask of port wine, some bottles of pickles, a few
> blankets, spoons & forks, two kegs of gunpowder, two parasols
> — not the most useful things saved — a small cleaver, a bucket
> or two, one tin of preserved meat ...*

Charlie added that there was also 'some wood, and a few odds
and ends thrown off the forecastle-head'.

Harold Turner specified that the salvaged spirits included
'two cases of gin, two of rum, one of brandy', and that there
were eight tins of jam — or 'confectionery' — in a case. He also
mentioned two sailor's chests, saved from the fo'c'sle: 'These
contained, among other things, about a dozen boxes of matches,
pipes, and a few pounds of tobacco, a Bible, and a writing-desk,
full of writing-paper ... The matches were rather wet, and to
dry them we rubbed them in our hair.'

The sailmaker talked of two tins of meat rather than one, and
the second mate clarified that the matches were Bryant & May's
Safeties. He also listed the ship's biscuits — which had been eaten
by Saturday — and a passenger's chest, which as well as blankets
and cutlery contained 'a sheet or two, a few tablecloths, napkins,
towels ...We also picked up a case of boots, which when we
opened on shore turned out to be ladie's [sic] boots of a very
small size, and not men's, to our great disappointment, most of

us being very poorly supplied with that article ... we also picked up a case of caster oil, which we afterwards lost.'

'There we were,' wrote Fanny, 'forty-seven men, one woman and a child on a barren rock and in these were our whole stock in trade.'

As the *Times* editorial went on to acknowledge, the *Strathmore* survivors were not nearly as well off as Robinson Crusoe: '... in the case of the *Strathmore* ... [Crusoe's] conditions were as nearly as possible reversed. Very little was saved from the wreck ... Nor did the character of that part of the Crozets on which they were cast do much to make up for the defects of their original stores. There were sea-birds, there were weeds, and there was water, but there does not seem to have been anything else.'

The most serious defect of Grande Île, from the survivors' point of view, was the lack of firewood — it was 'a barren rock, with a little rank grass on it,' wrote Fanny, 'there were no trees or shrubs of any description ... not even brushwood'.

How could they cook their seabirds and survive the cold without fire?

By the end of Saturday, 3 July, they did have better shelter, at least, than the night before, having finished the hut earlier in the day. The wall was built up to over a metre in height, but it was still not high enough to close the gap between it and the canvas boat covers. 'The inside we floored with flat stones,' wrote the second mate, 'and laid grass on top of them, to sleep upon.'

While the first hut was being completed, Black Jack and a group of sailors had been building their own shelter. They constructed it beneath another overhanging rock about six metres further up the cliff — 'the wall in the front being composed of stones and turf,' wrote Harold Turner, 'about four feet in thickness'.

EXTERIOR OF HUT

The survivors' hut, as imagined by the Illustrated London News

'About a dozen of the men built a shanty a little higher up than ours,' wrote Charlie. 'A sailor called "Black Jack" ruled it — and a capital ruler he made, too.'

The third mate saw things differently. 'The bad characters seemed to keep together.'

But young Harold concurred with Charlie's estimation: 'I and most of the crew were in "Black Jack's" camp, so called … from the man who was the chief … [he] had a very swarthy complexion, but … was as thoroughly good-natured and as generous as any sailor who ever stepped aboard ship …I preferred living in this camp, because the occupants, with two exceptions, were sailors.'

At the meeting that afternoon, the survivors agreed that Black Jack's men would come down to the 'Lower Shanty' for meals, so that one cooking fire would do for both camps.

'We had to be careful with the fuel we had,' wrote Harold Turner, 'and therefore could not afford more than one fire.'

Most of our time is spent hunting for food

Every year, large numbers of penguins, albatrosses and other seabirds arrive on the Crozet Islands to breed. The birds are attracted by huge schools of krill, drifting on the currents formed by the Antarctic Convergence, that great meeting of cold Antarctic waters with the warmer seas of the sub-Antarctic ocean.

Seabirds were the main source of food for the *Strathmore* survivors. Their ship was wrecked in July, the depths of the southern winter. No penguins had arrived yet on the Crozets. A group of albatrosses — probably wandering albatrosses — was getting ready to leave the island after breeding.

'At this time,' wrote Charlie,

> *the food we lived upon was young and old albatross; the young ones gave more eating than the old, being large, heavy birds, with a beautiful white down upon them about three inches long. They sat in nests built in the grass about a foot from the ground, one young one in each nest ...*
>
> *The albatross were very majestic and graceful in their movements ...*
>
> *Another bird that we lived upon ... [were] 'stinkpots,' a carrion bird. They were ... heavily-built birds, with fierce, strong beaks. I remember getting a bite from one that hurt through a pair of Wellington boots, trousers, and drawers. They seemed to stay on the island all night, and we caught them by chasing them into rough ground, or into gullies, where they could not easily get on the wing, and killed them with wooden clubs. They would face you when brought to bay; the albatross seldom did.*
>
> *We used to see these stinkpots feeding on floating substances in the water, very likely the bodies of our unfortunate shipmates. But that did not deter us from eating them, even half-cooked as*

they sometimes were; the very thought of that food now almost
sickens me.

The 'stinkpots', or Antarctic giant petrels — also known to the
survivors as 'greybacks' — were named for their habit of spitting
a foul-smelling substance at their predators. '[W]hen chased,'
wrote Harold Turner, 'the "Greyback" … would turn round and
vomit its food over its pursuer, in order to stop his progress, and
to enable it to run the faster'.

There were also a few great-winged petrels (the men called
them whistlers) and a small but permanent population of Crozet
Island sheathbills — Charlie called them 'the real owners of the
soil: the only unwebbed-footed birds of the island, and constant
residents … what we called "little white thieves", "white pigeons",
or "white crows"'.

Although the survivors knew the ocean around them must
be full of fish — far more appetising food than seabirds — they
had no way to catch them without boats.

'We never knew what fish inhabited these waters,' wrote
Charlie,

> *for it was impossible, on account of the quantities of seaweed*
> *and the constant swell of the sea dashing against the rocks, to*
> *keep anything that we could make for a line clear enough for*
> *fishing; and what made it worse was the height any likely place*
> *was from the water.*
>
> *We used to see parts of fish in the big gut of the albatross*
> *when they had their young to feed. I remember once killing*
> *an albatross, and, as was often the case just before dying, it*
> *vomited up the contents of its bag, and amongst the mess*
> *was an eel quite perfect, and having the appearance of being*
> *cooked.*

> *I took it up and ate it, and it tasted quite like stewed eel. I daresay that was the only fish eaten on the island.*

There were seals too, just as impossible to reach.

> *The seals we used to hear barking like dogs at a distant hamlet; it sounded so pleasant, for we could imagine ourselves near some village ...*
>
> *We never could get near these seals, as they frequented places unapproachable to us. One day a huge beast ... having a head like a bear and the body about ten feet long, was seen to attempt a landing, but, on second thoughts, it dived into the depths again. I suppose it was a sea-lion. I have seen several of what appeared to me large seals swimming about, but perhaps they were all sea-lions.*

Harold Turner 'often saw sea elephants and any number of golden seals ... [we] were unable to reach them or we might have changed our diet a little'.

For the first six weeks on the island, all the survivors could add to their diet of wild birds were the roots and greens they found growing among the rocks. 'The only thing we had in the shape of vegetables,' wrote Fanny, 'was a sort of moss with a long root which tasted something like celery and when there was no root, we eat [sic] the moss itself.'

'There were some green things,' agreed the third mate, 'like carrot tops, and a sort of clover with a taste of cress, and a bitter kind of cabbage.'

According to Harold Turner, the survivors 'ate the tops of a plant we called carrot, and grass for herbs ... The upper portion [of the carrot-like plant] looked like the tops of carrots; the root, which was about the thickness of a penholder, crept along the surface of the ground.'

Vegetables, the survivors knew, must be eaten to prevent scurvy, but albatrosses and other birds were their main food.

Getting enough birds to keep forty-eight people alive was a big job, and an exhausting one. Just over a week after landing, the second mate made the following entry in his journal: '9 July. Wet and miserable. Nothing particular doing; only caught enough birds for food, which little piece of excitement wears out our strength, and we gradually get weaker; but we trust some ship will take us off here, which hope keeps our spirits up.'

Though the albatrosses were huge and very strong, they were easier to catch than the stinkpots, being less aggressive. But they nested higher up, and climbing the steep cliffs to the nests was exhausting and dangerous, especially when the rocks were slicked with sea-spray and rain.

The hard work of chasing the birds over rocky terrain and beating them to death was made harder by gale-force winds and sleet. And the sheer volume of food needed each day required long hours of hunting.

'We spent most of our time in hunting for food,' wrote Harold Turner. 'Our clubs for killing the birds were made from the boats' oars, doubled round with hoop iron ...'

The task of finding food was made even more difficult by inadequate clothing and footwear — some of the men had to borrow boots before they could go hunting. And there was a shortage of able-bodied hunters and gatherers. The survivors had been exposed to severe cold during the night of the wreck and for several days afterwards, and according to Fanny, 'nearly all the men were suffering from frostbitten feet ... the odour was something fearful'.

Over a quarter of the survivors were effectively disabled after just four days on the island, according to the second mate's diary: '4 July. There are today about twelve of us laid up with frostbitten and swollen feet, and of course they are no good for doing any hard work, or hunting birds.'

Although the temperatures during the early days of July were bad enough to disable over a dozen men — and had contributed, perhaps, to the death of George Mellor — in fact the survivors were lucky with the weather.

'The first week was mild in comparison with those that followed,' said one first-class passenger. 'We appeared to have arrived at the beginning of winter, and suffered much from ice and snow.'

If the wreck had been just a week later, there would surely have been many more deaths. As it was, the cold grew steadily more severe, bringing heavy frost, sleet and snow.

'We seldom washed our-selves,' wrote Harold Turner, 'on account of the water being so very cold.'

That which troubled us most was the inclemency of the weather, the wind at times blowing so strongly that we were almost unable to stand on our feet. This, with constant showers of sleet and snow, made things more unpleasant. The shanty wall would often blow down, and then we were obliged to leave our blankets in the middle of the night, and go among all the snow, to build the wall up again. We often had to do it, shivering in our wet clothes till they were dried.

The deteriorating weather increased the survivors' desire to get off the island, and kept them always watching for a sail. The first Sunday after the wreck, Peters had 'sent two parties out to erect two flagstaffs, going with one of them myself'.

One group used the mast from the lifeboat, sinking its lower end into the turf on the island's eastern peak. The other men took an oar up to the western summit, propping it upright with stones — though the winds there proved so strong they later took it down.

The pool of possible hunters was further reduced by the effort to watch for and hopefully signal to passing ships. Much time was spent repairing flagstaffs and flags damaged in the high winds, and, unless visibility was extremely poor, two men were always on lookout duty. It provided a break from the exertion of catching birds, but standing still in the freezing winds near the flagstaff was such cold work that most preferred to hunt.

Both the weather and the work were relentless. Each freezing morning Black Jack, Charlie and the other thirty-odd hunters woke up knowing not only that they had to kill enough birds to feed themselves, but that they must also find at least half a day's food for an invalid or lookout man.

The hunters had to feed Wattie and Fanny too, though neither of them could eat much of the coarse, fish-flavoured albatross flesh. 'I was too ill to eat more than barely kept me alive,' wrote Fanny, and 'poor little Wattie Walker ... was more dead than alive.'

Fanny was able to drink her small tot of hot grog after dinner, however — a mix of spirits and water heated over the embers of the cooking fire, and carefully served out by the second mate.

'We ... used ... the wine and spirits we saved ... very economically,' wrote Charlie, 'a small salt-cellar full of wine or spirits-and-water being served out every night till finished, except a bottle of rum and one of wine, which were buried for the use of the sick.'

Both Fanny and Wattie managed to down their share of the seawater-diluted Keiller's jam, which was rationed out and eaten soon after landing, freeing the empty tins for use as cooking pots.

'Our mode of cooking was primitive in the extreme,' wrote Fanny. 'The birds, albatross and "stinkpot" alike, were skinned, cut up and boiled in Keiller's tins, and so long as the pickles lasted they were minced and put into the water the birds had been boiled in, the result being a very palatable soup.'

'There was little of the birds that we did not find a use for,' added Charlie, 'even the entrails were roasted and eaten, and the large guts we stuffed with chopped-up meat, and tried to imagine them sausages; but there was no such thing as anything with a taste on the island, except the soup when plenty of salt water was put in it.'

Collecting the salt water was a difficult job — the men had to wait for a gap between waves before rushing down to the water's edge. Water containers were sometimes lost in the process, as Peters' journal records: 'We had the misfortune to lose two buckets today in the attempt to get salt water, which we use at every meal, putting it amongst the water we boil our meat with, so that it has some sort of taste.'

Some of the invalids were able to help with the laborious work of skinning and cutting up the birds, and tending the cooking fire. They boiled the meat in relays — there were not enough tins to do it all at once. Most of the men ate their meat off the tops of their caps — though, according to one third-class passenger, Charlie and Fanny were served on tin plates — and they drank the soup straight out of the jam tins.

The survivors ate just two meals a day, partly because it was too much work to prepare three, and partly to spare their fast-shrinking store of firewood.

One day, wrote the second mate, 'The sailmaker found a piece of oak, about two feet and a half long, seemingly a piece of oak branch, but how it came there is a mystery, it being found some hundreds of feet above the level of the sea. It is the first piece of wood we have found since we have been here, except what we brought ourselves … Our stock of wood is very limited, and I see no possible means of getting more.'

All our firewood gone

Two weeks passed, and the weather grew colder.

'We have never seen a sail since we landed on the island,' wrote the second mate, 'and most of us [are] getting pretty downhearted.'

He kept track of the date and the days of the week in his journal: 'July 17. Still blowing strong, with thick weather. A sharp look-out kept as usual. Being Saturday, we all that were able caught birds enough for today and tomorrow — being Sunday.'

One of those unable to catch birds was the 22-year-old clerk and steerage passenger, Edward Stanbury. His feet had been badly frostbitten during the wreck. They became infected with what the men believed was lockjaw, or tetanus. The infection spread up his legs, which became so tender that he screamed from pain if anyone touched them. His flesh began to rot.

Stanbury was gravely ill. Peters 'used to give him wine two or three times a day; he could not take much else'.

'We carried no doctor,' said one of the passengers.

'There was no-one there,' added the steward, 'who understood medicine.'

According to a saloon passenger, the infection was 'caused by … [covering] his feet … [in] albatross skins with the flesh inwards'. Apparently many men got bad blisters from warming their feet with skins still hot from the bird. 'We got sore feet from using skins to cover them,' said a third-class passenger. 'Mine got very bad from using albatross skins.'

Whether or not the bird-skins caused the trouble, Stanbury was certainly in a bad way that Saturday, 17 July. 'Lockjaw having set in this afternoon,' wrote Peters, 'he is not expected to live long.'

On Sunday the island was beset with violent gusts of wind and heavy snowfalls. The survivors in the lower shanty stayed inside, singing hymns and trying to keep warm.

'Stanbury still hanging out,' Peters reported, 'the only nourishment he is able to take being a little port wine. We can all see his hours are numbered.'

Charlie spent the day trying to breathe through his mouth — Stanbury's feet were 'in a horrible state of corruption, and the odour from them and from the other bad feet was most offensive'.

Finally, about three o'clock on the Monday morning, 19 July, Stanbury died from what Peters called 'lockjaw, resulting from diseased feet, they being nearly rotted off'.

They buried the body as fast as they could: 'We dug a grave for him in the morning, and buried him towards evening, reading a chapter out of the Bible over the grave. Mortification having already set in, we were afraid to keep him any longer above ground … I am afraid more of us will soon follow, if not quickly relieved.'

Wattie Walker was probably uppermost in Peters' mind as the survivor most likely to die next. The little boy was still crying for his ma, the drowned Alice.

The firewood continued to dwindle. By the end of the first month on the island, according to Peters' journal, only a few days' fuel remained. '28 July. Cold weather, with constant showers of sleet and snow, which don't look very cheering, as our only chance of getting off is our having clear weather, so that our signals may be seen by some passing ship, which [we] are all the more anxious should be soon, as our small stock of firewood … is nearly exhausted …'

With no wood, wrote Fanny, 'we should have no fire to warm us, and the birds must be eaten <u>raw</u>'. Everyone dreaded the idea of eating uncooked albatross: 'We don't half like the thought of eating raw bird's flesh,' wrote Peters.

Charlie, 'contemplating the prospect of eating the meat raw', began to experiment and make plans: 'I ate two small birds raw, and a piece of another, by way of accustoming myself to it; but ugh! it was bad … [In case of] our being obliged to eat the meat raw, I … arranged a dish for my mother of minced liver, heart, and "greens" (the moss that I have mentioned), seasoned with gunpowder as a substitute for salt …'

As well as more exposure to cold, and the horrible taste and texture of raw meat, running out of fuel meant facing long hours of darkness.

Since early July, when they'd rigged their first lamp out of an empty bottle, each shanty had kept a light on all night. Charlie described a lamp made 'out of a piece of tin, and a wick out of the cotton padding in coats'. For fuel they 'scraped the fat off the skins, [and] melted it down into oil'.

Nights on the island were usually windy and full of loud noises, and the shanty walls were prone to collapsing in stormy weather. Wattie was not the only one who found a night-light comforting. Peters called it 'a great improvement, as we have found about fifteen hours' darkness every night …'

With no fire, there would be no way to make lamp oil, and nothing to keep the darkness at bay.

At last, Friday, 30 July, the final stick of wood was burned up.

'… when that was done,' wrote Harold Turner, 'we had no more, as there was not even a single tree on the rocky island'.

The day was comparatively mild, according to the second mate — 'pretty clear at times' — but there were no ships on the horizon. 'We … have been trying experiments with turf, but owing to everything being saturated with rain it is impossible to get it to burn.' Charlie remembered the turf 'smoulder[ing] slowly, and that only when there was a strong draught'.

In Harold Turner's memory the survivors went days without any fuel, and were 'obliged to eat the raw flesh'. According to Peters' journal, however, they went just one day without fuel: '31 July. To-day completes the month since we landed here, and it is a very gloomy day with us, as our firewood is all done, and all our attempts to cook a meal, failures until well on in the day …'

Fanny took up the story at this point: '… after turf had been tried unsuccessfully we were giving it up as a bad job when a man threw a bird skin on the smouldering fire and to our delight it burnt famously …'

As Harold Turner explained, a bird-skin fire needed careful tending: '… we … found that the skin of the albatross would burn almost as well as wood; but it required that one person should always be kept at the fire all day long'.

'An ordinary housewife,' added Charlie, 'would be rather puzzled to keep up a fire with bird-skins — it requires experience.'

The relief of having found a new source of fuel was tremendous.

Charlie: 'So here was this difficulty bridged over …'

Peters: '… it… raised our spirits greatly'.

Fanny: '… so long as birds lasted we were sure of a fire & that we might always have a light …'

Days without food

In the first weeks after the wreck, the residents of the lower shanty woke in the dark each morning to sing hymns before the hunters set off.

'Forever with the Lord!' they sang.

Amen! so let it be,
Life from the dead is in that word,
'Tis immortality.

Their voices rose and fell against the noise of wind and waves:

The darkness deepens;
Lord, with me abide …
Help of the helpless …

After learning how to burn bird-skins, according to the second mate, the survivors 'split partnership, thinking we should be better independent of one another'. As Harold Turner explained, the sailors from Black Jack's shanty were hunting for themselves, and: '… no longer got our food cooked at the mate's camp … [but] took "turn about" in cooking and looking after the fire, lest it should go out. We made soup of the salt sea water, the tops of a plant we called carrot, and grass for herbs. The water we had to carry in a pair of Wellington boots.'

Each morning, the sailors were woken at five by the strains of the day's hymn drifting up from below.

There is a fountain filled with blood,
Drawn from Immanuel's veins,
And sinners plunged beneath that flood
Lose all their guilty stains.

For a day or two after achieving their independence from the lower shanty, rather than rolling over and stuffing their fingers in their ears or joining in the singing — and perhaps they did not know the words — Black Jack and his mates immediately dragged themselves from their warm covers, racing to lace up their boots, grab their clubs and get out into the icy darkness to start hunting. But the morning singing soon stopped when the men from the lower shanty realised they were giving their competitors a head start.

'There was great rivalship between the two shanties,' wrote Charlie,

> ... one striving to steal a march on the other by getting up before daylight, which was very cold work, having to grope our way in the dim light of the moon or breaking daylight over the frozen ground, with mere apologies for shoes, generally struggling against a high wind, for it was nearly always blowing a gale in that bleak quarter of the world, with snow, hail, and rain to make it worse, and our inner man very indifferently replenished ...

When they first landed, the island, in Peters' words, was 'well stocked with birds' — mainly albatrosses. His diary entry for 4 July notes: 'We had our evening meal of young albatross, white crows, and what we call greybacks, which we devoured with good appetites ... We all keep up very well, Mrs Wordsworth in particular showing herself to be a true woman, refusing any dainties firmly, unless we all had our share of them.'

Less than two weeks later, things had begun to change: '15 July ... Caught a lot of birds, but found they were getting very scarce.'

The albatrosses may have begun to leave the island at this date, the adult birds and mature fledglings setting off on their great journeys across the southern oceans. But whether the birds were leaving yet or not, the newly arrived predators must have had a massive impact on their population. As Harold Turner put it, 'It was natural enough that their number — about two or three hundred — would diminish among so many hungry people. When the albatrosses became scarce, we took to catching and eating grey-backs, which also were very scarce.'

Young Wattie found any form of seabird meat too chewy. Subsisting only on thin, greasy soup, and suffering from diarrhoea, he lost weight. He stopped asking for his mother, now crying only for 'oop, oop' — his word for soup.

Fanny couldn't eat the bird-flesh either: '… at that time I could only take a little soup … The wine and spirits we had saved now became invaluable …'

Weak from lack of nourishment, she grew more and more unwell. Though Charlie encouraged her to eat what meat there was, he had little success. 'The coarse, rank flesh which was our continual food soon disagreed with her,' he wrote, 'and she got very ill with a sort of low fever, and a dreadful bowel complaint …'

Weeks passed, and the numbers of birds continued to dwindle. The weather did not improve either, as Peters' journal makes clear.

Very cold frosty weather … heavy falls of snow, which completely covered the ground.
Blowing hard, with cold weather …
… blowing strong, with thick weather.
Squally, with heavy falls of snow.
Foggy, constant rain.
Heavy fall of snow during the night and snowing occasionally all day, with a bitterly cold wind which penetrates through our clothes …

*Blowing a gale with heavy falls of snow, which was hard
frozen towards evening.
… constant showers of sleet and snow …
Dirty weather and miserably cold …*

Out in the wind, the temperatures regularly dropped well below zero, and even inside the shanties, Peters reported, the survivors were not safe from the weather: 'During the night there was a heavy fall of snow, and a part of our hut blew down.'

Everyone craved fat in the freezing conditions. In the lower shanty, hungry men stole so much of the bird-grease fuelling the night-light, that a 24-hour watch had to be kept over the lamp.

The remaining 'greybacks' — alias stinkpots or Antarctic giant petrels — began to get wise to the ways of the hunters, and harder to catch. '[The] birds,' wrote Peters on Monday, 2 August, 'are getting a good deal shyer than they used to be a few weeks ago.'

On the following Monday, 9 August, the food supply became a little more diverse, if not more plentiful, when two greybacks' eggs were found, 'which after being fried, we fancied were the sweetest morsels ever we tasted'.

The birds continued to lay throughout the week: '11 August to 25 August … The greybacks, which we live chiefly on, have been laying eggs this last eight days or ten days, so that some of us have had a slight change of diet occasionally, which is rather acceptable …'

There were not enough eggs for everyone every day, but the men gave them to Fanny and Wattie whenever they could. Hunters like Black Jack and Charlie would have had at least a small share of the delicious fat-fried eggs: '… the eggs were good,' wrote Charlie, 'and saved my mother's life, for at that time a few mouthfuls of the soup we made was all that she could take of the former food'.

As well as being strengthening for the sick, and a relief from the monotony and bad taste of bird-flesh, the eggs were comforting. Unlike the fish-flavoured meat and strange plants, they tasted blandly familiar to the homesick survivors. They reminded Wattie, perhaps, of nursery meals back in Birmingham. But there were not enough of them to make up for the lack of birds.

'It is very difficult,' wrote the second mate, 'to catch birds enough now to satisfy our hunger …'

At twenty-two years of age, Peters was very conscious of his responsibility as the senior surviving ship's officer. He must have been gravely worried at this time, but he did his best to look on the bright side — 'as yet we have never been really starving … we are all very thankful for our continued allowance of food, which seemed to be nearly all done about four weeks ago; but

Second mate Thomas Brown Peters, senior surviving officer of the Strathmore, *in later life*

… we have never had less than two meals per day, which has been our rule since we landed here …'

Some of those meals were getting very small, however, and the survivors were greatly afraid of them shrinking further. Powerless to change their situation, many turned to religion for solace, during what Fanny called 'this … most miserable period'. Third-class passenger Robert Aitkenhead Wilson and his brother David, the second steward, were among those who prayed, sang hymns and read from their one Bible. Whenever possible the survivors caught two days worth of birds each Saturday, so they could keep Sunday as a day of rest. Toward the end of the month, their prayers were seemingly answered, at least for the moment.

'We were very short of birds,' wrote Peters in a journal entry for the last six days of August,

> *but before dark we had a fresh stock again, and that of a kind we had never seen before. They are something like an albatross, but smaller, and they seemed to have just been sent when we stood most in need of them.*
>
> *We sighted a few small icebergs today, which was welcome as something new, and because it is a sign that summer is drawing near.*

But the survivors' relief was only temporary. Just a day later, Peters noted, food was shorter than ever, and the icebergs were no longer so welcome: '… we saw a large iceberg float into the bay, about a mile to the southward of the shanty, and there touched ground, where it stuck fast, which did not make us feel any warmer, as the wind blew from the direction of the iceberg'.

Over the next few days the hunters found it very hard to catch anything. 'Some days we were without food altogether,' wrote Harold Turner, 'other days we were obliged to be content with one meal.'

'The only thing we had to eat when we could not catch any bird,' said one of the sailors, 'was a sort of grass like the tops of carrots.'

'On a cold morning,' wrote Charlie, 'you might have seen us scraping the snow off the ground, and tearing up the root with our benumbed fingers, often too hungry to take the whole of the soil off the root, eating everything ravenously, dirt and all.'

As they grew thinner, the men's eyes appeared to bulge, and their cheekbones protruded from their faces. The bigger men grew alarmingly skinny. Their muscles wasted and their clothes hung loose.

Even when everyone was hungry, the sailors continued to look after Fanny. 'John Evans, A.B.,' wrote Fanny, referring to Black Jack's old shipmate, who'd walked from Shadwell to Leadenhall Street with him back in March, the day they'd signed on to the *Strathmore*,

> John Evans, A.B., or 'Old Jack' as we called him, one day when food was very scarce, brought me a small duck roasted, which he had been lucky enough to kill and get cooked.
>
> Though starving himself, he freely gave me this delicacy, and insisted on my taking it. It requires a person to be under similar circumstances in order to appreciate such self-sacrifices as I have mentioned.

The duck was probably a sea-duck, or Crozet Island cormorant. Despite such special treatment, Fanny became dangerously ill. She was suffering from a ferocious diarrhoea, which, as Charlie wrote, 'reduced her to a perfect skeleton, and made her so weak that I had to turn her in the night when a change of position was needed'.

Later, Fanny tried to describe her altered appearance to her daughter. 'Had you seen me at first you would not have known me … my eyes sunken and hollow, with a wild burning light in them horrible to see; my skin white and like a dead person's, my hands transparent, my hair short, and my figure gaunt, tottering, and with a dreadful stoop.'

Perhaps Charlie had told her about the wild light in her eyes, though he didn't mention it in his own description.

Wattie was in a bad way too. 'Mr Walker's child, Wattie, suffered dreadfully,' wrote Charlie,

> he was a lively little child, and talked on board the ship, but nothing but moans and whimpering could now be got out of him, and his little body was covered a good deal with sores; he seemed to have shrivelled up — his knees drawn up to his chin, his bony shoulders up to his ears, and about the size and weight of a lean turkey …
>
> He would only take a drop of soup, and that [only] from one of the quartermasters called Bill Vyning, an American.

'Bill, the quartermaster, a sailor of the right type,' added Harold Turner, 'attended to … [the child] with great care, nursing it and feeding it alternately with its father.'

Bill the quartermaster was foul-mouthed Yankee Bill, the man who'd got drunk with Black Jack on the night the boats were lost. Like several other sailors named in survivors' accounts as 'quartermasters' or navigators, Bill's presumably superior skill as a steersman was recognised only informally. He'd shipped as a plain able seaman, receiving the same £3 5s monthly wage as Black Jack and all the other able seamen.

According to the ship's papers, William Vining (also spelt Vyning or Vinning) was thirty years old and had previously shipped on the *Santa Rosa*, a Liverpool-registered vessel. American or not, his birthplace was listed as London.

According to third-class passenger Robert Aitkenhead Wilson, Bill was prone to bragging and to losing his temper. Wilson also remembered him as a hard worker and tough as nails. In the evenings, pulling his disintegrating gumboots from his raw and bloody feet, Bill's comment was: 'Well, boys, as my old mother used to say, it's hard but honest.'

There are no records of anyone else taking special care of Wattie. His father, Alfred Walker, 'was a weakly, handless sort of person who suffered from ill-health'. It was Yankee Bill who 'nursed' the little boy, and earned his trust — no-one else could get the child to eat. No doubt Wattie owed his continuing survival to this rough man.

The increase of our larder

On the first Saturday in September, according to Peters' journal, the hunters could barely catch enough birds for that day, let alone a double helping to cover the whole weekend: '4 September. We tried hard to get enough birds to last over tomorrow, but we were unable to do so, as very few birds were to be seen … It is still blowing stormy, with very cold weather, which we are unable to keep up heat for.'

On the Sunday morning, the hunters broke the Sabbath to go looking for birds, but did not catch any: 'Out early in the morning, but were unable to find many birds. The kind we had been living on for the last thirty or forty days [the greybacks or stinkpots] seemed to have left us altogether, and what are visible being so shy that we could not get near them …'

Weak with hunger, exhausted and demoralised, these habitually stoic men and boys began to show signs of strain.

'One day on the island,' wrote Fanny of that hungry Sunday, 'when food was scarce and hunting hard ... Charlie was fearfully low-spirited ... he was quite worn out and burst into tears. Poor fellow! I felt that more than anything that happened to me.'

Charlie describes the day like this: 'We got very hard up for anything to eat at one time; one day there were only one or two mollyhawks for our last meal, and Black Jack's tent had had nothing to eat all day. We were very weak and low-spirited. I felt as if all the moisture in my joints was dried up, and I fancied I could almost hear them creak as I dragged myself along. It was with a heavy heart I went out to hunt ...'

When he left the shanty, according to Fanny, Charlie was crying. He continued the story: '... instead of climbing up the hills, I went down by the side of the island, where I remembered to have seen a large quantity of nests, built of mud, smooth and round, about a foot from the ground, looking at a distance like the turrets of a small castle.'

Harold Turner described each 'turret' as 'a most ingenious nest of mud, almost perfect in shape, as if it had been cut out of a piece of stone ...'

The cliffs on which these nests were built, wrote Peters, were 'composed of crumbling rock, which, if you are not very careful will break off under your feet and launch you into the sea, a distance of some hundreds of feet'.

'Down the rocks I went,' wrote Charlie, 'and saw to my great delight, a quantity of beautiful white birds ... we afterwards discovered their real name was mollyhawk ... I killed about fourteen of these, as they let me come quite close to them, when I knocked them down with a club. They even flopped down among my feet. I carried about half of my prize down to the tent … Many of the others went out …'

As soon as they saw the 'mollyhawks' — most likely grey-headed or black-browed mollymawks — the hunters rushed down to the nests, where, in Peters' words, 'Sunday as it was, we killed between three and four hundred of them, knocking them down among the rocks …'

According to Harold Turner, the mollyhawks were slightly larger than geese.

> … they literally swarmed in in hundreds. They were just like a swarm of bees … When they settled, there was a general rush to see who would get them …
>
> Some would fly against us, and others would try to settle on our shoulders. All hands were now at work. On the Sunday, we killed in all about five hundred.
>
> The birds did not seem to know what to understand by the reception we gave them. They would stand staring at us, and would not move till we knocked them down … One portion of the island was quite white with the birds — I should think there were thousands of them.
>
> … that day we did nothing but eat after the birds were caught.

Charlie also remembered gorging on bird-flesh: '… great was everyone's delight and astonishment at the increase of our larder … Such a feast of tails we had … That appendage was cut off close to the back, the long feathers pulled out, and being burned for a time in the fire, was considered a great delicacy, and one of the perquisites of the hunter.'

Once more, the survivors felt their prayers had been answered. As Fanny wrote later: '… these beautiful white birds

… were a great treat & there being plenty of them our spirits were quite revived … Just when everything seemed at the worst something always turned up.'

And this time, their good fortune had come to stay, at least in the form of sufficient food: 'Things now began to mend …'

After the arrival of the mollymawks on 5 September — over two months after the shipwreck — the survivors did not run short of food again.

The hunting men felt the effects of the larger meals right away: '… we all seem to be enjoying pretty good health …' wrote Peters, 'meat at present being plentiful'.

The sailors in Black Jack's hut favoured mollymawk fry-ups. 'For frying-pans,' explained Harold Turner, 'we used the hollow stones, in which we fried the flesh of the birds. The fatty part of the birds, when fried and the liquid extracted, made a very savoury dish, which we called "cracklins": for these there was a great demand.'

By mid September, Peters was writing in his journal that 'the strange flock of birds that came here about a fortnight ago have begun to lay eggs, so that we are now pretty well provided for in the way of food'.

As before, the eggs were a boost to Fanny's health, and over the next few weeks she grew stronger, though it was a slow process.

> *The eggs saved my life twice …*
>
> *For the first three months on the island I could not walk a yard without assistance, even through the shanty. It was all rock and slippery stones, and the least wind blew me down. When I got a little better, Charlie would take me out a few yards and I returned myself. If no-one was about to give me a help, I generally crawled on my hands and knees.*

At around the same time that the mollymawks started laying, the survivors began hunting for muttonbirds, referred to by Fanny as 'curious animals' which 'were capital eating and by far the best food we had'. The muttonbirds, Harold Turner explained, 'lived generally in the ground, much as rabbits do in England'. Their nests, Peters added, 'have the island perforated like a honeycomb'.

Charlie called the muttonbirds a 'great and *real* delicacy'.

We found the young, but never, I think, the old ones, who seemed most mysterious birds. Their nests were under the ground, and to find them we had to stamp about till we discovered a hollow place, our feet very often going right through the surface into their nests, when we had only to put in our hand and pull out our treasure. They had a delightful flavour, and were covered with beautiful fat.

We also had whale-birds, divers, and what we called 'the whistlers', from the noise they made. All these smaller birds lived in burrows underground, something after the manner of the muttonbird. The whale-bird laid, I think, two eggs of a delicate pale colour: the little diver's egg was noted for its size compared to its own bulk.

We were visited also in great numbers by a ferocious brown hawk; they were most audacious birds, and if their nests were interfered with, they attacked with vehemence the trespassers. The underground residents, whale-birds and divers especially, were wofully [sic] preyed upon by these hawks; the latter would stand patiently for hours near their burrows, like keen terrier dogs watching a rat-hole, ready to pounce upon the unwary who ventured from their fortresses.

The hunters competed with the hawks to catch the burrowing birds. 'One day,' wrote Harold Turner, 'as three of the men were on one of the hills, one of the number threw a club at a hawk, but unfortunately missed his aim. Although the club was very heavy, being wrapped at one end by wire, the hawk picked it up by its beak, and flew off with it some distance over the sea, and then let it drop, when it immediately sank.'

The survivors soon grew used to having enough to eat: '… in fact,' wrote Peters, 'some of us are getting fat, meat at present being plentiful'.

Harold Turner noticed that the abundance of food did not tend to make the survivors more observant in practising their religion. 'Some of the passengers were in the habit of reading the Bible and singing hymns and psalms, when there was a scarcity of birds; but when they became plentiful, they soon ceased to "read and sing" … I regret to say that the Bible was not read very much; [though] it was certainly read more on the Sunday.'

Heads & thraws

At around five and a half metres long by two and a half metres wide, the lower shanty remained far too small for the thirty-six people crowded into it. For two and a half long months, each resident had had an area of just one metre long by thirty-eight centimetres wide to sleep in.

'We passed a scrambling sort of night,' Peters wrote on one of the very first nights — 4 July — 'being compelled to lie almost piled on top of one another …'

'About 30-odd of us crammed in here,' wrote Charlie, 'lying in tiers on and between each other's legs; and it was not for months after that this horrid crowding was remedied by building other shanties.'

It is true that people were generally shorter in the nineteenth century, and Wattie did not take up much room. Edward Stanbury's death would free up extra space, and some time before the end of July three more passengers moved into a new hut. Still, the little shanty was bursting at the seams.

Packing the men into place each night was a feat of engineering, as one third-class passenger described: 'Now the word would be for a long thin fellow to go well under the cliff, then perhaps for a small man to jam in some cranny at the immediate risk of breaking his neck, or to be used as a wedge to make all taut.'

Once they were all squeezed in it was hard to move. Many were suffering from what they called dysentery, or diarrhoea, and were compelled to go outside during the night. No doubt they stepped on their neighbours' arms and legs as they struggled from their places, climbing over tightly jammed bodies all the way to the door.

The nights were long, and anything but restful. 'Here we lay,' wrote Fanny, 'in our wretched hovel endeavouring to forget our miseries in sleep … we lay … in the old Scotch fashion "heads & thraws" … Think of this ye mothers wives & daughters & try and realise what a pleasant situation it was for a weak sick woman.'

In fact, Fanny had more room than the men — they gave her 'a very small mattress of dirty shavings', which must have been salvaged from the ship. But no mattress could spare her from the stench of unwashed bodies and rotting feet, or from the unstoppable plagues of lice that kept the survivors scratching day and night.

'We seldom could clean ourselves,' wrote Charlie,

the dirt was too fast on us to allow of water alone taking it off, and the weather was so bitterly cold that we could only dabble a very little in it … we had a mode of cleaning our faces a little by means of bird's skin, rubbing ourselves with the greasy side first, thereby softening the dirt, and afterwards rubbing that off with the feathery side.

Our clothes were black with smoke and very filthy, and we were crawling with vermin, which we could not get rid of.

The shanty roof, made of canvas and calico, was prone to ripping in the wind, flapping about 'and bringing down about our ears part of the wall', as Peters put it in his journal. Even when the roof and walls stayed up, still the weather got in — 'our roof was … no protection against heavy rain, although it might keep out the dews which fall sometimes at night.'

The shanty, agreed Charlie, was

by no means water-tight … to say that our sleeping-places were damp would be a mild expression; we often lay in downright slush, composed of wet grass and dirt, with the rain coming down on our faces … My mother, it is true, had a mattress, but that was sodden and rotten with the moisture, and, from its clammy and wet feeling, was most disagreeable to touch.

In such close quarters, and under such dismal conditions, the survivors got on each other's nerves. Second mate Peters, who had taken on the role of leader, was a natural target for discontent. During the daytime, when the able-bodied men were out hunting or up at the flagstaff keeping a lookout for ships, the invalid men had the hut to themselves, aside from Fanny and Wattie. There were generally about a dozen too ill to work, mostly third-class passengers sitting huddled under blankets.

Though Fanny was the only woman on the island, and though there must have been some sexual frustration (and perhaps activity) among the men, it seems clear that she experienced no sexual threat. The sailors were unfailingly chivalrous toward her, and no doubt would have protected her by force had there been any necessity. She apparently felt quite safe in the company of her male hut-mates, and certainly had no qualms about speaking her mind to them.

'In the mornings after Mr Peters had left the camp with the other working men,' wrote Fanny later, 'I often heard the others unjustly murmuring at and abusing him, and I often indignantly asked why they did not abuse him to his face … No doubt he and all others lost their tempers; in such a place and under such miserable circumstances it was no wonder, and all were more or less selfish. I judge by my own feelings what I saw around me.'

The invalid men were perhaps likely to complain of Peters, since they were generally given the less favoured sleeping places, and got smaller meals than the hunters.

'At first everything was divided,' said the third mate, 'but not properly, for those who had sore feet got but little. What we saved of the liquor was left in charge of the second mate, but those who were strong got more than the weak.'

'The sick,' said a saloon passenger, 'who were unable to work, got but little to eat, the second mate saying that the working men should have the most.'

'Here is the explanation of that,' countered Peters. 'There were several who feigned sickness for the purpose of avoiding the rough foraging work of running down and killing the birds, who nevertheless managed to despatch them as fast as any of us after they were cooked, and our only cure for such a disease was putting them on short allowance.'

'The conduct of the second mate on the island,' said invalid passenger George Crombie, 'was not such as to deserve praise.'

'I certainly had no thought then of working for praise,' wrote Peters later, 'nor do I desire it now. I challenge Mr Crombie to say what it is he refers to. Meanwhile, I rather think that the cause of his wail is that we declined to forage for food for some who were as able to provide themselves with it as we were.'

Fanny, who was always treated well by Peters, thought the invalids' gripes against him unfair. 'He took all the care that was possible of the sick ...'

She did allow that meals had been unjustly served out during the first weeks: 'While the cook and steward had the management of the food, I believe it was not fairly divided; but after Mr Peters and the engineer, John Nicholl, managed the cooking and distribution of the food, all allowed it was fairly and honestly done.'

She had little sympathy for those who protested against Peters' rule.

> Many were not sick, but lazy, which left all the work to be done by a few. And then food was scarce, and hard to get; and it was generally allowed that those who worked so hard should get anything that was over after the distribution of food.
>
> Mr Peters showed great forethought and prudence all along, making rules and regulations which were partly kept; but of course after a short time everyone declared themselves their own master, and would not obey him ...

'The second mate,' declared a third-class passenger, 'appeared to me to be afraid of the men.'

'There are various other statements,' wrote Peters, 'which have appeared regarding myself ... [They] are so vaguely stated as to bear different constructions, and therefore are unworthy of further notice.'

Fanny's description of the lower shanty implies that her mattress was close to Wattie's sleeping place: 'The best corner of this delightful habitation was given to poor little Wattie ... and myself ...'

Like the men, Wattie slept on armfuls of wet grass laid over stones. Except when his father or Bill took him outside to expel streams of almost liquid diarrhoea, his days were spent curled up in the foetal position, shivering and moaning. He was probably in considerable pain from his festering sores and empty stomach. His old life of active play, regular meals and reliable maternal affection had disappeared completely.

Like his son, Alfred Walker — that 'weakly, handless' Birmingham stockbroker — was ill, and in the early stages of grieving his young wife's death. He knew very little about the care of small children. Yankee Bill was out all day hunting, and though clearly a kind and practical man, he may not have known much about children either. Men were not expected to look after them in Victorian times.

Fanny, who had mothered offspring of her own, probably had more experience of infants than anyone else on the island. Did it ever occur to her, as she lay listening to Wattie's whimpering for weeks and months on end, that she might take part in the care of the small boy lying just a metre away?

She was often ill during this period, of course. But at times she had a certain amount of energy. According to one of the third-class passengers, she found Yankee Bill's constant swearing so distressing that she would sometimes leave the hut. And when something really moved her — like criticism of Peters — she found the strength to at least speak out about it. We know from Peters that she made efforts to think of others: '... refusing any dainties firmly, unless we all had our share of them'.

She may have been incapable of helping with Wattie's practical care, but his needs for comfort and affection, for maternal love, were at least as great. Did she ever consider giving the little boy a cuddle?

Perhaps Fanny, ill and exhausted, lacked the emotional energy to care for the boy. Perhaps she was not good with children. Wattie, it must be said, was not an appealing child at this period. He was miserable and unresponsive — 'nothing but moans and whimpering could now be got out of him'. He was skinny and dirty, covered in weeping sores. He stank of urine and faeces. Yankee Bill 'nursed' the little boy, but he was more used to dirt than Fanny, and perhaps less aware of the danger of infection. The germ theory of disease was becoming more widely accepted in the early 1870s, and the Wordsworths may well have feared Wattie's sickness.

Also, Fanny, Bill and the other *Strathmore* survivors saw children somewhat differently from how we see them today. The notion that a child deprived of physical affection and stimulation will suffer cognitive, motor and social retardation was not current.

And even if some of the survivors did realise the effect of emotional deprivation on the little boy in their midst, they probably thought retardation was the least of his worries. The adults around Wattie expected children to die. Child mortality may have been sad, but it was all too frequently inevitable. Fanny herself had lost three babies, and she was not unusual. Children died in the most favourable circumstances, let alone in conditions harsh enough to kill grown men. If Fanny, in her weakened state, did consider reaching out to the little boy, the belief that Wattie was dying may well have undermined her impulse. Perhaps caring for an ailing infant was simply too painful for her after the deaths of her own children.

If it is remarkable that Fanny took no responsibility for looking after Wattie, then it is equally remarkable that none of the men, as far as we know, said she should have done so. This may have been because they thought Wattie a lost cause, or because Fanny was clearly too ill. Maybe they did not want to criticise, maybe they did not want to dwell too much on Wattie's plight, or maybe the subject did not interest them.

In the meantime, Wattie persisted.

'The child was sick,' said a first-class passenger, 'and used to cry a good deal.'

Without exercise or activity during the day, Wattie slept fitfully through the long, wedged-in nights. Hour after hour, the little boy lay in the tangle of men carpeting the hard floor, sandwiched between Alfred Walker and Yankee Bill, 'his knees drawn up to his chin, his bony shoulders up to his ears'.

Falling in and out of consciousness, did the child switch from dreams of Alice and sago pudding to the snores and murmurs of the men, the billow and thwack of the hut's canvas roof, the roar of the wind? Sea crashed on the rocks below, and the cold damp must have seeped into his bones.

All night long, threading in and out of sleeping and waking, there was the stink of the hut: faeces, pus, damp clothes, stale sweat and wet grass, the ammonia scent of the guano in the hut's front wall, the reek of burning bird-fat from the lamp.

All night long, the lamp burned. Whenever the survivors woke they could see the dim light of the little flame flickering across the uneven clods of turf in the wall and the hollows and projections of the rock overhang. Sometimes the flame went out and there were hours of darkness to wait through — loud and cold and cramped and foul-smelling — till at last the morning came. They would send someone up to Black Jack's shanty, where the sailors, in Charlie's words, 'would most likely have a light, so we got ... [the lamp] rekindled without reducing the stock of our precious matches ... we had only half a boxful of Bryant and May's safeties'.

The 'horrid crowding' in the lower shanty drove the men to start work on new huts as early as mid August. Finding time and strength for building cannot have been easy with empty bellies and long hours of hunting in the severe cold.

'As we are rather close packed in our cave,' wrote Peters on 25 August, 'there are two other[s being] … prepared for sleeping in, so that when the weather gets a little warmer we won't get stifled.'

By September, with conditions beginning to improve, the survivors found more energy for hut-building, as Charlie recalled: 'The weather was now getting rather less severe … [though] we could only recollect three fine days all the time we were there, and we always had to pay dearly for them. Our larder being always supplied with the new birds, we began to look about us more …'

But it was not until the middle of the month — after several weeks of enough food — that the first of the huts was ready, as Peters recorded on 22 September: 'During this last week six of our number went away to a new hut they had been building, which leaves us a little more room in this one.'

'Another shanty was being built,' added Charlie, 'and I was promised a very small old one for my mother and myself, which a third-class passenger had previously built, and … kindly offered us.'

A great luxury

Although the survivors now had enough to eat, they were starting to run short of fuel again. By mid September, Peters was complaining that the mollymawks and 'other birds are getting so lean that we can scarcely get enough fat to keep our fire burning during the day and our lamp during the night'.

But just days later, 'in the nick of time', a new kind of bird arrived in the Twelve Apostles. 'About the end of September,'

Charlie wrote, 'the penguins first made their appearance. They are a most remarkable set of birds, if we may call them so; for they have no wings, but just flippers, and their coats look more like fur than feathers; in fact I think them not unlike seals.'

'They are a kind of mixture between a bird and a fish,' added Harold Turner. 'They live chiefly in the sea … [and] have web feet and a head like a bird, with seal-like flippers.'

These strange creatures were probably macaroni penguins, which breed abundantly in the Crozets. At first the penguins came ashore in small numbers — one or two a day, none for a few days, then half a dozen. But by 29 September they were arriving en masse.

'During the last week,' recorded Peters, 'some hundreds of penguins have landed on the island, for the purpose of breeding, I suppose.'

The birds soon began to build their nests.

'It was very amusing to watch them,' wrote Charlie,

> … one would go to a little distance and pick up in its bill, with great ado, a small stone, and carry it with immense dignity to its mate, when they carefully arranged it in some mysterious way, shaking their heads and gobbling over it; then turned up their faces towards the sky and waved their flippers, as if asking a blessing on their labour or making incantations. A few stones thus got together constituted their nests: a single blade of grass or two I have seen treated in the same manner; but I never heard of them or saw them build in the grass, but always on stony places, often great heights above the sea.
>
> They made great fuss over their courting, and woe betide any unfortunate hen who dared to be frivolous, leaving its own nest to go [for] a short walk; for no sooner was it noticed, than all the neighbours raised a cry of anger and horror, and prepared to

give the delinquent an unmerciful pecking as it wended its way through the thick ranks of its comrades. If it returned to its lord and master, the tune was immediately changed from discordant howls and croaks to a more musical tone of thanksgiving and rejoicing.

Fortunately for the *Strathmore* survivors, the penguins had been storing fat for months before their arrival on the island, in preparation for breeding. The large, heavy birds were an excellent source of cooking and lamp fuel.

'We used to cut away the fat,' wrote Harold Turner, 'which was about an inch thick, to render into oil for our lamps ... The flesh was black, and when fried became very dry.'

Penguin-watching lent variety to the survivors' monotonous existence.

'The habits of these birds were very singular,' wrote Harold.

They would come up from the sea, marching in single file, and congregate together on the hillocks of stones. They divided themselves into two companies, which we called respectively the Prussian and French armies. I am sure there must have been several thousand in each company. Sentinels were perched here and there on high places; and if anyone was seen approaching, they would make a cawing noise, as a signal to the rest. We found these birds very useful in many ways.

The most useful of the penguins' habits was the laying of eggs. They began to lay in mid October, just a few weeks after landing on Grande Île, as Peters noted in his diary: '13 October. Today we gather the first of the eggs laid by the penguins, which have now landed on the island in their thousands, and still coming ashore as fast as they can land ...'

Unlike the penguins' flesh, their eggs were what one saloon passenger called 'a great luxury'.

'The yolk of these eggs,' added Charlie, 'boiled hard before the white, the latter looking like arrowroot when quite boiled, and also tasting not unlike it; but our palates were perhaps not to be depended upon after living so long on coarse, fishy food.'

The arrowroot Charlie was familiar with was a semi-transparent jelly; the 'white' of a hard-boiled penguin egg was see-through, a milky egg-shaped jelly with the bright orange globe of the yolk suspended in its centre. Harold Turner remembered the penguin eggs as 'about the size of a hen's egg', though they were probably somewhat larger.

According to Charlie, each female bird laid three eggs:

I have seen in books of natural history that penguins lay only one egg; now our penguins laid three. The first was the smallest, and of a light-green colour; the others whiter and larger, especially the last one. They all had strong rough shells, which, when ... nearly hatched, had been worn by constant friction on the stones smooth and thin, easy for the young ones to break through. The position of the bird when 'sitting' is upright, or very nearly so.

There were almost more eggs than the survivors knew what to do with.

Whilst the penguins were laying we had plenty of eggs, not only for the time, but for long afterwards, as I 'pitted' about a thousand of them for future use. Even my mother has eaten seven at a meal, fried, roasted, or raw, beaten up with a little fresh water, which made a most refreshing drink ... some of

them ate about thirty at a meal ... and we saw each other with
clean faces, for we used the eggs as soap ...

Peters' journal shows the men in the lower shanty jumping at the chance to get clean: 'The most of us have been busy these last few days washing our bodies and clothes, neither of them being very clean after three months and a half's wear; but as we have no soap, and the weather being so cold, we could do nothing towards cleaning ourselves, until the eggs got so plentiful, when we found that they were [a] pretty good substitute for soap.'

But the most important benefit of the eggs was as a source of nourishment for the hungry survivors. 'Those who had been haggard and miserable got quite plump and fresh,' wrote Charlie. 'The eggs did every one a great deal of good, and we all felt satisfied and had not the longing desire for other food.'

Charlie may have been overstating the survivors' satisfaction. 'We are now almost entirely living on penguins' eggs and young mutton-birds,' wrote Peters, 'but we would willingly exchange the eggs for potatoes.'

According to Charlie the unusual diet had some unexpected effects: '... a most remarkable thing was, that every one had fair skins and light hair, dark faces and hair being quite changed — black hair turning brown or red, and fairer people quite flaxen. As for myself, my complexion was pink and white like a girl's, with white eyebrows, yellow hair and moustache.'

Black Jack's hair and beard must have lightened with the rest — perhaps the sailors called him Red Jack or Mouse Jack for a while.

Fanny disliked Charlie's new colouring: 'From the effects of the exposure and bad feeding on the island, his hair ... got quite flaxen, which didn't suit him at all ...'

Her own complexion was not much affected, and though the eggs improved her health, she remained weak and underweight: 'My mother did not change much ... she was a mere skeleton and very feeble.'

Nobody recorded the effect of the eggs on Wattie.

Penguin Cottage

Though not strong, Fanny was now well enough to move out of the overcrowded hut.

'Some more of the men left the lower shanty,' wrote Charlie,

and my mother and I got installed in our new abode. It was high up on the hill at the other side, on one of these stony shelves frequented by the penguins ...

The tracks that the penguins made through the grass wound up round the edges of cliffs; they were narrow and stony, and had the appearance of having been worn down to their present condition, through the soil and grass, by the tread of countless penguins seeking every year their favourite resorts, which must have been their choice for ages. Some of these paths in places were very steep; and really, to look at the rocks they managed to climb up, you would think they would require a ladder ...

We had to force our way through a dense cloud of ... [penguins] to reach our hole, which we called Penguin Cottage ... [It] was made by building a turf wall against a slanting piece of rough rock ... The wall was about four feet wide, built of sods; but not having a spade, tearing up these sods with our hands made them very uneven, and gave lots of channels for rain to find its way through ... Of course I plastered up these places with mud as well as I could, but to little purpose ...

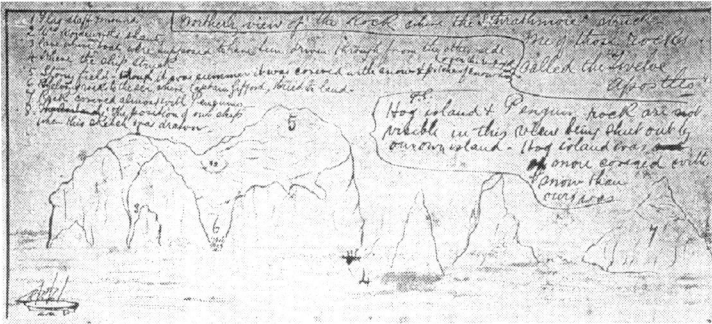

Some landmarks of Grande Île, from a sketch by Charlie

Of all the huts that had been built — about six in total — Penguin Cottage, according to Harold Turner, 'had the most extensive view of the sea'.

The Wordsworths were greatly relieved to get away from the bickering and overcrowding in the lower shanty, and Fanny's health continued to get better: '... when we got to our own little hole on the other side of the island, I got rather stronger, and was able and proud to go to the spring for water, escaping with only two or three falls ... On my way to the well I passed through crowds of penguins without fear. I think they were surprised at my appearance.'

Although Fanny and Charlie were grateful for the privacy of Penguin Cottage, the hut itself was no improvement on the lower shanty. It was tiny and very damp. Inside, as Fanny explained, it 'was about four feet in the highest part and about five feet long, besides this there was a shelf of rock about three feet wide & five feet long which we used as a bed but as the foot was always in a boggy state the length was materially diminished'.

'The bottom of this bed we called the "well",' added Charlie, *for the damp was so great that our coverlet would get as wet as if dipped in muddy water; consequently we kept our legs curled up, which took away from the width. When both were in the shanty, one often retired to bed to make more room, we were so crushed; besides, one side not being water-tight was too wet to sit down near, and we had to crouch under the rock to keep out of the rain …*

In the wall of our little shanty there was a whale-bird's nest. They were very quiet; but before rain they cooed and moaned in the most plaintive and musical tones, and after that you never had to wait long for wet weather.

'Our furnishings were limited,' wrote Fanny, '& our house consisted of a very small mattress of dirty shavings, a counterpane, a table spoon, <u>plated</u>, a teaspoon <u>real</u>, a fork, two bottles (great treasures) a small piece of tin, made into a frying pan about six inches long & about one deep, a stone lamp, two stone frying pans, a fire place, & two or three umbrella wires.'

Inside Penguin Cottage—the somewhat romanticised view of the Illustrated London News

These umbrella wires — no doubt taken from one of the parasols salvaged from the wreck — were, as Charlie explained,

> *used for pokers, or bars to rest the tin pan on … The most*
> *valuable articles in the cabin were my club and knife: the latter*
> *was simply invaluable — no money would have bought it;*
> *without it I could not have kept up an independent shanty, and*
> *upon it and my club depended every necessary of life. Another*
> *useful article was a needle made from the wire of an umbrella.*
> *The thread we used was unravelled worsted …*
>
> *I had quantities of oil got from the fat of the penguins put*
> *in the large gut of the other sea-birds, also in what we called*
> *'pigs' — that is, the skin of a penguin without a cut in it, dried*
> *and made a bag of. They were also used for carrying water.*
>
> *When we first went to our own shanty, I generally went*
> *down to one of the other shanties for boiled meat and soup; but I*
> *afterwards gave this up, and depended entirely upon myself …*
>
> *We managed to have a fire as there were lots of penguins,*
> *though we were not very good at keeping it alight till we got*
> *accustomed to it. The way we managed was this: At night before*
> *the fire was quite out, I put in a piece of dry turf, which kept a*
> *spark in, or got red-hot through, and lasted, if a good piece, till*
> *morning. I then put dry grass or shavings from the mattress and*
> *blew it till it caught, or helped it with gunpowder, then hung*
> *strips of fat skin over the flame, thereby making a good fire …*

'On a [very] rainy day,' wrote Fanny, 'we generally staid in bed as it saved fuel and not much could be done.'

'This was the usual daily routine,' explained Charlie,

> *from which the reader will be able to form some idea of the life*
> *we led: I got up about seven o'clock and took the ashes out of*

the fireplace, lit the fire, and swept out the house with a bird's wing. When the stone pot got heated, I put in the grease, and if we had eggs, we fried them in it, or cooked the meat in it. It generally took about a couple of hours to cook the breakfast, as we could do so little at a time: my mother looked after it sometimes.

After breakfast I often went down to the gully and had a wash …

'Our washing was peculiar,' wrote Fanny, 'in fact <u>very</u> peculiar; when eggs were plenty we used to use about a dozen as soap but when we could not afford eggs we cut a penguin's throat over a piece of rag and scrubbed ourselves with the blood, then washing it off with water.'

Penguin blood, according to Charlie, 'was not such a good plan as the eggs, but was better than nothing'.

'It wasn't nice as you may fancy,' commented Fanny, 'but it was better than being dirty as we were.'

'My wash over,' wrote Charlie, 'I would get birds for our evening meal, either young penguins or mollyhawks, and then set to work skinning and cutting them up … After that I generally killed and skinned about fifty old penguins, and stored up the skins for winter fuel.'

Fifty penguins a day is three hundred penguins a week, allowing for Sundays. How many penguins were killed on the island in total each week? The death toll went down in bad weather, and not all the men worked as hard as Charlie. Men on lookout duty had less time for hunting, and the invalids killed no birds at all. But even if only ten men were killing at Charlie's reported rate, up to three thousand penguins were dying weekly — as many as fifteen thousand a month.

The birds were quite easy to catch. They could not fly away,

Fetching water in penguin-skin 'pigs', as imagined by the Illustrated London News

and at first they were without fear, being unused to human predators, though eventually they learned to understand the danger. 'After a time the penguins showed fight,' said one first-class passenger, 'and came at us with their beaks.'

Though not hard to get near, the penguins were, in Peters' words, 'very bad to kill'. A skilled hunter could slay an albatross with one blow, but a penguin could stand a great deal of belting about the head before dying. Even after the most ferocious beatings they might jump up and march off again. 'The penguins are plucky creatures,' wrote Charlie. 'I have even seen a weak, soft-looking youngster stand up manfully for itself …'

After some practice, the men learned to stun the birds with a smart blow to the beak, before wedging them belly up between their knees and simultaneously slitting their throats and breaking their necks.

Charlie's take on the ongoing penguin massacre was largely utilitarian, entirely untainted by 21st-century notions of conservation and animal rights. He recorded neither concern for possible long-term effects on the penguin population nor distaste for the slaughter of individual penguins. From the survivors' point of view the mass killings were an unpleasant but necessary business.

> *Thirty fat skins were about as much as a man in our reduced state could carry easily. I packed them in stacks about four feet high. The old-kept skins burnt well, though they smelt strongly, and were full of maggots; but we were very glad to have them. I had stored about 700 or 800, which would have lasted us some time, as we only burnt about five or six in our small fire during the day.*
>
> *I was always glad to get my skinning over, as I had got so sick of it; and dreadful-looking figures we must sometimes have been — our hands and clothes covered with blood, and our faces often spotted with it.*

'What a mess that skinning business used to make of him,' wrote Fanny, 'none of his old friends would have recognised him.'

The evening meal, according to Charlie, 'was generally cooked by my mother, of which I ate some, leaving a little for the morning, then got in water for the night, put the turf on the fire, and retired to bed, or rock rather. I generally slept well, except when I dreamt of skinning penguins. My mother also slept pretty well, considering the discomfort, &c.'

The men left behind in the lower shanty were sleeping better too — they had more room to stretch out in once the new huts were occupied. After the Wordsworths moved up to Penguin Cottage, just fifteen survivors remained in the big hut. Yankee Bill was still there, and so was Wattie.

Killing penguins, as imagined by the Illustrated London News

The wild, reckless life

By mid October the survivors were dotted about the island in separate camps, as Harold Turner described.

> ... these camps were distinguished as follows: — 'Lower Shanty', occupied by the second mate, Bill, the quartermaster, and several others; 'Sea-View Terrace', so called on account of the view of the ocean from the camp. It was often called 'Black Jack's Camp', from the man who was the chief. Here I and twelve others lived. I preferred living in this camp, because the occupants, with two exceptions, were sailors. 'Flagstaff Villa', situated near the flagstaff, was tenanted by the cook, steward

*and several passengers; 'The Hermitage', a nice little cave on
the highest part of the hill, was not wholly occupied, as it
was too far up the hill, and quite out of the way; 'Freemason's
Lodge' was inhabited by the third mate and several passengers;
'Pleasant Valley Cottage', situated in a pretty picturesque
valley, was occupied by the boatswain and several passengers;
'Mud Cottage' was obliged to be abandoned, on account of its
insecure condition; 'Penguin Cottage' had the most extensive
view of the sea, and here it was that Mrs Wordsworth and her
son Charles lived.*

Though less crowded conditions made things easier, there were
still tensions between the survivors in the different huts.

One conflict was between Black Jack and the third-class
passenger Robert Aitkenhead Wilson over some information in
Wilson's diary. Black Jack had learned from Sails, who'd asked
Wilson to read aloud from the diary as an entertainment, that
the diary included the initials of all the sailors who'd been logged
for breaking into the *Strathmore*'s cargo. Potentially, this was
evidence that could be used against the men back in England.
Wilson probably wrote the names in the ship's log himself, in
the course of his secretarial work for Captain MacDonald.

Shortly after talking with Sails, Black Jack went after the diary.
He and his mate Funny Lad followed Wilson and the third mate,
Allan, as they left their hut to go hunting one afternoon. Jack and
Funny Lad came up to the two men and started a conversation,
making small talk about when a ship was likely to rescue them.

In the middle of this, Wilson reported, he heard Black Jack
say, 'Allan!' — a warning to the third mate to step aside. Jack and
Funny Lad then grabbed Wilson, wrestled him to the ground,
ripped open his jacket and seized the diary from an inside
pocket.

'Black Jack and Funny Lad took it from me,' said Wilson. The two men told him they would give the diary back. Jack then took the book to Peters and asked him to read it aloud. 'The second mate,' said Wilson, 'afterwards read it to the crew.'

According to Wilson, he asked Peters if he could rip out the offending pages, not wanting the whole diary to be destroyed. After checking with Black Jack, Peters told Wilson that the book would be given back intact. But Wilson never saw his diary again. 'When I asked for it,' he said, 'I was told it had been burnt.'

Black Jack allegedly said there was enough evidence in the diary to get him put away for two years, and that he wished he'd thrown Wilson into the sea. The sailors were so angry with Wilson that some passengers were afraid he would not get off the island.

For his part, Peters hotly denied that he'd sided with the men against Wilson. 'Mr Wilson says: "The second mate read his private diary to the crew," which I did not. The matter stands thus: Black Jack, as he has been called, brought a note-book and asked me to read it for him, which I refused to do after I found out what it was. I returned it immediately, and never afterwards saw it.'

Possibly due to the feeling against him, Wilson later ran into more trouble, this time with Yankee Bill and his mate Dutch Charlie.

A fashion war had broken out in the lower shanty, begun when the second mate and sailmaker embroidered their caps with the Dundee Clipper Line flag, perhaps out of pride in their status as ship's officers. Provoked, Yankee Bill and Dutch Charlie decorated their clothing with their own flags — presumably the Stars and Stripes and, maybe, the Norwegian flag — (since 'Dutch Charlie' was most likely the Norwegian sailor Hans Eriksen).

Yankee Bill decided he wanted to complete his outfit with the brass buttons of Wilson's reefer jacket, and one morning Dutch Charlie went to fetch the buttons for him. Finding Wilson on lookout duty, Charlie attacked him, and tried to tear the jacket from his back. They scuffled, and rolled partway down the hill. In the end, Dutch Charlie swapped his own coat for Wilson's and gave Yankee Bill the two or three brass buttons that remained.

Black Jack was also involved in a sartorial dispute, though it's unclear whether fashion or function was the issue. A full-length black frockcoat that he'd salvaged from the *Strathmore* was at first distributed to the invalid George Crombie, though Jack said it was his and threatened to repossess it. Eventually he did take it, sewed a big sailcloth pocket on the front, and went 'stalking about' the island in the modified garment, black cloth billowing in the wind.

In the survivors' struggle to keep the bitter cold at bay, cooking equipment was easily as important as clothing, and as collective property it tended to spark more serious disputes. The precious Keiller's jam tins — used for cooking the soup which helped the men thaw out after hunting — were distributed among the different camps.

'Every party,' explained the second mate, 'as they leave [for the new huts] get a share of what things we had saved from the wreck. Our pots, which are only confectionery tins, appear to be good as ever, and considering the work they have to do — being on the fire from daylight until dark — one would reasonably have supposed that they would have been worn out by this time.'

It was not long before the tins did begin to wear thin. The pot at Black Jack's camp was the first to fall apart. According to Robert Aitkenhead Wilson, the men in Flagstaff Villa feared that the sailors would take their pot as a replacement. About a fortnight after the breakage, some of Black Jack's men turned up at Flagstaff Villa and began picking a fight.

Afraid for their prized pot, the Flagstaff Villa men took it down from its place. Straight away the sailors seized it too, arguing that it belonged by right to the larger group. Just as the pot seemed about to break, Black Jack appeared, threatening to demolish the hut and take everything in it.

Wilson and his friends gave in. '[They] took our pot from us,' he said.

Black Jack gave them the pieces of broken pot in exchange, to use as frypans. '… they took a pot from us because we were weak,' said another Flagstaff Villa resident. 'The strong men took from the weak …'

For some of these 'strong men' — the ones who could not be pushed around — life on the island at this time was not so bad, if one believes Harold Turner's somewhat inconsistent account.

> *We all tried to make ourselves as comfortable as we could, and, to a certain extent, succeeded … Not having much trouble in catching birds, we made ourselves very content under the circumstances … we began to care very little whether we were taken off the island or not. Indeed, we were quite accustomed to the wild, reckless life we were leading, and our only care seemed to be to provide food for our daily subsistence …*

The idea that any of the survivors experienced contentment on Grande Île is hard to swallow. Imprisoned on the island, far from friends, family and home, their lives were severely circumscribed. They may have had enough food, with the arrival of the penguins and their eggs, but their diet was at best monotonous, and conditions in the flimsy, overcrowded shanties were appalling.

Their shelter and clothing were not nearly good enough to protect them from the freezing winds and constant wet.

Nonetheless, Grande Île probably did not seem as bad to Black Jack and the other sailors as it did to first-class passengers like Fanny and Charlie. The sailors were used to living hard. They'd been on ships where the meat was rotten, the flour full of weevils, the water foul-tasting, where rations ran short toward the end of the voyage. They'd sailed for weeks on end through storms and icy weather, unable to keep dry or warm. And even on good ships in fine weather there was no privacy.

No-one likes to be trapped in a place without means of escape, but the sailors were at any rate familiar with confinement — there's no getting off a ship in the middle of the ocean. And for them, life in the Twelve Apostles had one great advantage over shipboard life: freedom from discipline. They paid little heed to the second mate, and with no captain or first mate to tell them what to do, no threats of flogging or being clapped in irons if they disobeyed orders, the men were able to do as they pleased.

All the *Strathmore* survivors had to adjust to their situation, whether they liked it or not. To some degree their changed habits affected their way of being, altering their thoughts, their attitudes, even their speech. 'If we stop here much longer,' wrote Peters, 'we will soon have a slang language of our own, which strangers would not understand.'

Life on Grande Île was harsh, and the survivors' entertainments were limited, but camaraderie was strong, at least among Black Jack's men. They worked hard, but they also liked to sing and joke around, and were always telling yarns.

Unlike Harold Turner, Charlie Wordsworth was never in danger of becoming contented with his lot on the island. Perhaps he'd have had more fun living with the sailors, who liked him, according to Fanny: 'He won the respect of all, especially the sailors, with whom he was a great favourite.'

But up at Penguin Cottage Charlie saw little of the other men, and generally had to wait until Sunday for masculine conversation.

> *On Sunday I never did any skinning, but washed myself in the gully in the morning. We always had a supply of food ready for the Sunday.*
>
> *I then paid visits to some of the other shanties, and got all the news, such as a new yarn; and dreams were a great source of amusement — we dreamt in such a realistic manner. Having dreams was quite like a letter by post, for they took our minds off the island, and enabled us to forget for a time our miserable circumstances …*

'These dreams,' added Fanny, 'and the sailors' "Yarns", Charlie used to retail to me … and wonderful some of these dreams were… what do you fancy the dreams were about? generally <u>something to eat</u> — especially <u>bread</u> <u>and</u> <u>butter</u>.'

'In the night when we woke,' wrote Charlie, 'we invariably asked each other's dreams, which were often about something to eat, often about being at home and the ship that was to take us off the island — always pleasant. Dreaming, in fact, was by far the pleasantest part of our existence on that miserable island.'

'Once,' wrote Fanny to her daughter, Fanny Rosamund, 'I had a delightful dream of your kitchen at Bebbington, full of lovely clean clothes airing before the fire. It was quite a treat to me, squalid, ragged, and cold as I was.'

But, as Charlie realised, there were limits to the comfort of dreams: '… though we had the most vivid dreams of home, &c., and things to eat, yet there was always a feeling in the background which dispelled a good deal the pleasure of the dream — at least that was my case; but still I looked forward to my dreams'.

Neither Charlie nor Fanny went into detail about the subject matter of the sailors' yarns, but one imagines tales of travel and adventure, funny stories told at the expense of others, and probably much bragging of sexual exploits — though this surely was not passed on to Fanny.

The sailors were not the only ones to tell yarns, Fanny later wrote to her daughter: 'In the evenings, when the day's work was done, I would amuse Charlie by telling him all the little stories I could remember about his own, your, and even my childhood, which took back our minds to home, and never failed to interest, however often repeated.'

Another rich source of yarns was the island's abundant birdlife. Many of the survivors were close observers of the various birds that frequented the Twelve Apostles. One of their favourite subjects for birdwatching was the Crozet Island sheathbill, described by Fanny as a 'curious little animal … a white pigeon with an extraordinary amount of vitality. It might be knocked down and just as you were going to pick it up off it flew.'

Charlie called the sheathbills 'little white thieves'.

They possessed many of the qualities of our jackdaw, being very inquisitive and mischievous, hardy, and not to be daunted by trifles. Their build was stronger and more compact than that of a pigeon, but they were about the same size. I do not think they were powerful fliers. Their feet and beak were black, the latter having a sort of wart on it about the nostril, larger in the male than in the female; whilst their plumage was pure white. Their eggs were dark and speckled.

These little 'thieves', when the penguins were on the island, never ceased watching them and their eggs. They would sit on a stone which gave them a commanding position over the multitude beneath, and wait for a chance of stealing an egg, and they had a very knowing way of bending down and putting their head on one side to see under the penguin's tail.

When a chance of robbing presented itself, they descended from their elevated position, fearlessly hopping amongst the crowded penguins, evading adroitly the pecks aimed at them, stuck their beak into the egg, and, if they had not time to enjoy it there, would open their beak whilst inserted therein, and lifting it in this way, would fly to their holes in the banks or rocks and demolish their cleverly-earned meal at their leisure …

Their chirrup sounded like 'Quick, quick!' which seemed to be their motto.

The Crozet Island sheathbill is the subject of the only recorded Grande Île yarns. According to Fanny, these yarns were told by Black Jack, though Charlie attributed them to Yankee Bill.

One of our men tells a story of one of these 'white thieves', who, tired of an unprofitable vigil, had the audacity to come quietly up behind a penguin sitting on its egg and impertinently peck its tail (a great insult); and when the penguin got up to resent the injury, the little rascal dabbed its beak into the egg and carried it off.

Apropos of their hardihood, an American sailor relates the following anecdote; but I daresay it requires to be swallowed cum grano salis. He had killed one of the birds, as he thought, and had sat down to pluck it warm; he had done so all but the wings, and had taken out his knife to cut the latter off, when away the bird fluttered minus the body-feathers.

Of all the birds on the island, surely the penguins were the most amusing.

> *Being always amongst the penguins, their habits were of great interest to us, and their noises my mother used to fancy resembled nearly all the sounds of the farmyard. A lot of them cawing at a distance seemed like the lowing of a cow; there was the cackling of ducks, the hissing of geese, the gobbling of turkeys, and even the noise of a donkey braying, to be distinguished amongst the babel of tongues.*
>
> *... The long lines of travelling penguins, meeting each other on their narrow tracks to the sea, seemed to be very particular about keeping their own side of the street. The homeward-bound ones, with their full paunches, laboriously climbing up the steep paths, and their funny little short legs, white bosoms, and black, extended flippers, looked like fat old gentlemen in white waistcoats; and one could almost fancy that you could hear them puffing and blowing with their hard work.*

In November, Charlie observed the preparations of the adult penguins for the hatching of their young.

> *When the penguins had been sitting some weeks on their eggs, a visible decrease in their numbers was noticed, and we thought at first that they were leaving us entirely; but the hens were left on the island, looking very lean and care-worn, whilst the cocks went to sea. This was the first time we had seen any of the regular householders leave their homes, even for food, since their arrival on the island; and whilst on shore they were never seen to eat anything. However, I think in a week or so the cocks came back, and very fat, there being about an inch thick of fat on their skins, which was very precious to us. Most of them,*

too, had their paunches full of a sort of food which did not look unlike a linseed meal poultice; this was for their young, which were either hatched, or very nearly so. The hens, when relieved by the cocks, then left for their holiday; but I do not think that they stayed so long away nor came back fat like their mates.

… Whether the penguins who had been out at sea always came back to their old mates, who had been left behind or not, I would be afraid to say. Yet I think sometimes they did; but their numbers were so great, and they were so much alike, it would be impossible to decide.

By mid month, the first of the baby penguins were emerging from their shells.

'We were much amused to find that some of the eggs began to hatch,' wrote Harold Turner, 'even in pools of water. The young birds were covered with a lead-coloured down, and consisted chiefly of stomach. They seem particularly tenacious of life; for if we threw one, say five or six yards, it would burst open, and almost immediately, it would pick itself up again and run away.'

The survivors found their entertainment where they could, but, as Harold wrote, their minds were always occupied by the hope of rescue: '… we were constantly dwelling on the thought that some day kind Providence would send us a deliverer, that we might again rejoice the hearts of those who were still hoping that we might again return to them'.

It was four and a half months since the wreck and still no ship had come for them, but they had not been entirely without signals from the outside world.

5

Rescue

When they first landed on Grande Île, the survivors hoped for a swift rescue: '… we trust some ship will take us off here,' wrote Peters on 10 July. But throughout the months of July and August, they saw no sign of a vessel. It was not for lack of trying, as Peters' journal makes clear. 'All anxiously looking for a sail,' he wrote.

One day there might be 'very foggy weather, giving us no chance of seeing far to seaward', while another day was 'pretty clear at times, but nothing hove in sight'.

Weeks of fruitless watching rolled by:

Two hands on the look-out all day.
Two hands sent to the look-out as usual, but had to come down shortly afterwards, they being unable to see the water.
… although the most of us kept a sharp look-out all day, we were not gladdened by the sight of one single sail.
… we kept a sharp look-out for a sail, but were not gladdened with such a long-looked-for sight.
… we saw no signs of a sail.
… not a single sail … hove in sight.
… two hands on the look-out.

... most of us are looking anxiously round the horizon for some signs of help; but evening closed in without our seeing anything like a sail.

... nothing in sight, although we are looking for something in the shape of relief.

'We sent several bladders over the cliffs into the sea,' wrote Harold Turner, 'containing a note telling of our perilous situation.'

The survivors watched for ships by day, and dreamed of them by night: '... our ... dreams,' wrote Charlie, 'were often about ... the ship that was to take us off the island ... Many were the prophecies that were made about when we should get off. At first we anxiously paid attention to them; but when one or two turned out wrong, no one took much account of them.'

Waiting for ships that did not come was depressing. 'We have never seen a sail since we landed on the island,' wrote Peters, 'and most of us getting pretty downhearted.'

The constant disappointment was particularly hard for the bereaved, already cast down by grief, and for the invalids, who were in pain, and cooped up in the tiny huts.

Twenty-year-old first-class passenger Thomas Henderson was both ill and grieving. He'd lost his younger sister, Maggie, in the wreck — the Miss Henderson who'd shared a cabin with Fanny, and been variously described by her as 'a weak minded pretentious idiot', or 'the poor child' who 'always tended me with the greatest kindness and gentle care'.

Maggie's brother missed her greatly. He blamed himself for letting her go when the sea washed her out of his arms.

'Mr Henderson and his sister,' wrote Peters,

both seemed to be in a very delicate health ... [Mr Henderson] could not eat the food ... [we] had to eat. He was also troubled

with sore feet ... from the day we landed he seemed to lose all
heart, and being by nature rather delicate, he has been nearly
all the time unable either to assist in hunting birds or otherwise
do any work about the huts.

For two long months the lookout men saw nothing but empty
sea. Then, as Harold Turner described, on the last day of August
a ship came in view: 'A man came running down the hill, crying,
"Sail, ho!" We picked up a blanket, and ran up the hill.'

'[I]mmediately we were in the highest state of excitement
and hope,' wrote Charlie, Peters adding,

[it] made the most of us run to the top of the hill as quickly as
possible; but we were disappointed when we saw the distance
she was from us, being in fact so far away that the most of us
could not see her at all ... She appeared to be standing to the
eastward, but we could not be certain how she was going or
what she was.

As Charlie wrote, 'it was a great deal too far off for them to see
us, or we to signal them'.

This ship was probably the *Helen Denny*, sailing from London
to Napier. Apparently the *Helen Denny*'s mate thought he'd seen
a fire on one of the Crozet Islands, but he assumed it was lit by
whalers.

The *Strathmore* survivors soon lost sight of the ship. 'A little
fog came,' wrote Harold, 'and she disappeared from view. Our
hopes were again gone ... One of the third-class passengers put
his hand over his heart, and began to cry, saying that it would
break his heart. We laughed at this, as we wished to keep up our
spirits as much as possible.'

'Seeing the ship seemed to have different effects on us,'

commented Peters, 'some it seemed to cheer up, although she was so far away, as we were beginning to think that ships did not sight these islands very often …'

According to Charlie, Thomas Henderson was the most profoundly affected by the ship's passing: 'Poor Mr Henderson, who had been ill and low-spirited since we landed, got worse. He had been ill with a never-ceasing diarrhoea which nothing could stop … His body was mere skin and bone … I daresay the raised hopes that had so suddenly come and gone with the ship were too much for him in his enfeebled state, and he died Sept 2d.'

Henderson was the third man to die on Grande Île.

'On account of the severe frost and bad weather,' wrote Charlie, 'we could not bury him for two or three days. His limbs up to the last were quite supple …'

In fact, it was four days until the weather cleared enough for grave-digging, as Peters' journal reports: '6 September. Today commenced with constant rain, which cleared away towards mid-day, when we dug a grave and buried Mr Henderson … Poor fellow, he was wasted away to a skeleton … I cut off some of his hair, which I intend to send to his friends when I get the opportunity.'

'We buried him on the island,' wrote Harold Turner, 'having first taken off all his clothes, as we could not afford to lose any … After the reading of a chapter from the Bible by one of our men, we closed up his grave, and there left the earthly remains of one who had proved himself a kind man and good companion under our unpleasant circumstances.'

Henderson's burial was on a Monday, and for the rest of the week, as Peters wrote, the survivors experienced the 'usual run of bad and fine weather which we have had since we have been on the island, bad weather predominating'.

On the morning of the following Monday, 13 September, the men in Black Jack's shanty stayed in bed to keep out of the cold, as Harold Turner described: '... the ground was covered with snow, and we were snug under the blankets, [when] we heard the cry of "Sail, ho!" from Mr Wordsworth'.

'I was in what was called the Skinning Cave,' wrote Charlie,

and saw the ship ... a full-rigged ship, under reefed topsails ... and gave the alarm first ... Away went some of us, as hard as we could run, with blankets and counterpanes to the flagstaff, our black figures showing well against the snow-covered hill, so that I believe they could not have helped seeing us.

'We immediately picked up a blanket,' wrote Harold Turner,

and ran up the hill, and attached the blanket to the lifeboat's mast, which we had previously fixed on the hill's summit ...

The ship was coming between the islands. We calculated that she would be about two miles away, as we could see her deck quite distinctly.

... the signal-blanket was blown to ribbons, the gale of wind being so strong. Beside this signal of distress, we each waved a blanket or some kind of clothing, in order to attract attention ...

'The blanket-flag was up in a very short time,' wrote Charlie,

and the ship, when she had got past the end of the island, came into the wind, I believe, for previously she had been running with the wind aft, and we all thought that she had seen us, and was going to stay for us till finer weather came to take us off, when a squall of snow came on and hid her from view.

The **Strathmore** *survivors signalling to a passing ship, as imagined by the* Illustrated London News

> She had gone off a little in the squall, but some of the men
> said she was still 'hove to'. She had not increased her distance
> much, but eventually she took to her heels … [and] we never
> heard anything more of her.

The ship, as one first-class passenger said, 'either failed to see us
or would not take pity on us'.

'He took no heed of our signals,' wrote Peters later in the day,

> although we were all sure that he must have seen them, if his eyes were not shut against seeing ... [but] he must have been in ... an excited state of mind at finding himself in so narrow waters, having come through between Hog Island and a lot of outlying rocks which stretch out from our island to Hog Island, leaving a very narrow channel for him to come through.
>
> It has been blowing a gale all day, with 'bursters' ...

The ship was the *White Eagle*. According to the *Auckland Herald* in March 1876,

> the ship was found entangled amongst breakers, with the wild peaks of the Crozets hanging almost overhead. By a special mercy of the Almighty she had plunged in the darkness through almost the only channel between the mass of rocks, and emerged ... into the open sea beyond.
>
> But, while passing an intricate strait, some of the sharp-eyed passengers said they saw signals flying on one of the islets. The officers of the vessel were too much occupied during their critical position to pay proper attention to the assertion, and in a short time the ... signals were shut out from view.

No-one reported the incident when the ship reached Auckland. Fanny had little sympathy for the *White Eagle*'s predicament:

> We afterwards learnt her name, and heard that some of the passengers had actually seen us and entreated the officers to wait for us but they refused ... Shame on them for ever; and it

must always remain a blot on the honour of British seamen that an English shipwrecked crew were left in danger by an English ship ...

'Now I am sure she saw us,' added Charlie,

and to desert us thus was abominable. She was near enough to let us see her topmast and topgallant and rigging; and when we could see all that, how could she not see our black figures and a large blanket and counterpane flying against a clear sky? Except during the squall the air was beautifully clear, and they must have had glasses, which we had not.

'Our disappointment,' wrote Harold Turner, 'can scarcely be imagined ...'

Around the time of the *White Eagle*'s passing, one of the older sailors fell ill. Able seaman William Husband, known as 'Daddy' or 'Old Nimrod', had left the wreck on the port lifeboat, along with Charlie and Fanny. He was a quartermaster and, in the words of one third-class passenger, 'an inveterate grumbler'.

Second steward David Wilson, older brother of Robert Aitkenhead Wilson and an invalid himself, took care of the old man. 'He was very dirty,' said Wilson later, 'and would not look after himself ... He had something the matter with his thumbs.'

'Wilson did nothing but attend to him,' said the second mate.

Throughout the following month, Husband grew dangerously thin. He was, said one first-class passenger, 'too old for the food they had', and by the third week in October, according to Harold Turner, he was 'almost wasted to a skeleton'.

By 23 October, William Husband was dead.

'He had been ill for weeks,' wrote Peters, 'in fact, he being an old man, was not very able to stand the hardships we have been exposed to, and he has never been well since we landed here ... The real cause of his death I am unable to state, but among his other complaints was that of frostbitten feet — one of his big toes being completely rotted off before he died.'

'The [mollymawk] eggs came too late for him, poor fellow!' wrote Charlie, 'but he gave himself up from the first. He always said most of us would get off, but not himself, and that our greatest chance of getting off was after Christmas ...'

Four of the survivors had died now, and the rest were wondering which of the invalids would go next.

'We were very much afraid,' wrote Charlie,

> *of our engine-driver, John Nicoll, or 'Steam', a nice cheery fellow, who was very delicate, and spitting blood in quantities. He was to have got the bottle of wine that was buried, but it was stolen — a great sin, for they knew it was for the sick.*
>
> *There was still a little rum left which did him good. (N.B. Get Henry White of London's 'Red Heart rum' if you want anything good in that line; it is medicinally better than brandy.)*

As far as we know, no specific accusations were made regarding the stolen wine, though Black Jack and Yankee Bill may have been suspected, after the loss of the boats.

It is not recorded whether any of the rum was given to Wattie.

Hope at the bottom of the casket

The weeks dragged by.

'Thus in the same routine our life passed on,' wrote Fanny.

'We kept an account of the days,' recalled Harold Turner.

'Several of us had watches, but each in its turn stopped, owing, we thought, to the damp.'

Watches were not the only possessions that suffered on the island. Footwear wore out especially fast. Hours of hunting over rough terrain in wet weather proved very hard on shoe leather, particularly as boots were shared, many survivors having come off the wreck barefoot or in slippers.

The first report of the shortage appeared in Peters' journal on 10 August: '… our supply of boots is still getting scarcer. I suppose we will have to run barefooted by-and-by.'

'To save our shoes as long as we could, we used to wrap birds' skins round our feet,' recalled Harold Turner, 'but these temporary shoes lasted only a day.'

Before long, bird-skins were the only foot-coverings available, as Peters reported.

> 19 October. All our boots are done long ago, and we make penguin skins into things like boots, sewing them with canvas threads, or worsted taken from our comforters or stockings. Penguin-skin boots are a poor substitute for that article, and only wear from one to three days if we walk about, the rocks being so rugged they soon cut them all to pieces.
>
> Our clothes are also getting very ragged, and we are all heartily tired of our banishment from civilised society.

'Our clothes wore out very quickly,' wrote Harold Turner, 'and these we knew not how to replace …'

'Some of us had to make penguin skins into clothes,' said first-class passenger Frederick Bentley. 'Most of us had penguin-skin caps.'

'[S]uits of clothes,' added Harold, 'were made from the feathers of the albatrosses.'

'We are such queer-looking figures here,' observed Fanny.

Bird-skin outfits looked strange, but according to Harold they had an important advantage: 'The ... skins we used for shoes and clothing ... being of a close nature, were very warm.'

Various materials were used for sewing equipment. 'I made two needles of the wire from the rigging of the lifeboat,' said Frederick Bentley.

'... for thread we unravelled our stockings, jerseys, and canvas,' wrote Harold Turner, '[and] finding a parasol in one of the chests, we made needles from the wires ...'

'We cut them off below where they meet at the top of the umbrella,' explained the third mate, 'and sharpened the ends. These enabled us to sew our penguin skins together. At first we took threads out of canvas, but subsequently grass was used as a thread.'

'We adopted several ingenious methods of improvising necessary articles of use,' wrote Harold Turner. 'We made knives from the hoops of the boats' kegs ... When our hair wanted cutting, it was cut with a knife, the operation being more painful than pleasant.'

Another ingenious improvisation — jam tins for saucepans — was fast coming to the end of its usefulness, as Peters reported:

We are now cooking in all sorts of articles, only two of the confectionery tins being in fit condition to boil meat in, and those two of course being in the biggest huts — the other huts having to fry their meat on the sides of the old tins, or in stone frying-pans, which can be picked up on the island after a diligent search.

Stone frying-pans are only stones hollowed out so that they will hold a little fat to fry the meat with, and of course we have

to find them hollowed out by nature, as we have nothing to
hollow them with.

In Harold Turner's words: 'Truly, "necessity was the mother of
invention" with us in a thousand ways.'

As their few possessions wore out, the survivors kept their
spirits up however they could: '… hope at the bottom of the
casket,' wrote Fanny,

> *was never quite extinguished.*
>
> *One day … brought something out of the common. It was*
> *the first of November and I was sitting at the fire side when a*
> *head and face appeared to me. It was a beautiful face, pale with*
> *dark eyes and a kerchief was tied over the head and under the*
> *chin. It smiled kindly on me and then disappeared.*
>
> *… the remembrance of that angel's face was ever present*
> *with me. Remember I had not seen a woman's face for months.*

Charlie retailed Fanny's vision to his sailor friends: 'I told some
of them about it, and it was soon all over the island …'

By mid September, British newspapers were reporting the
Strathmore missing. 'Much anxiety is felt in Dundee regarding
the safety of the fine ship *Strathmore*,' said the *Liverpool Mercury*
on the twentieth. 'She has now been five months at sea, and
vessels of similar size and equipment that left later have made
the voyage in from 70 to 80 days.'

Before long, the papers were speculating on the ship's fate.
'It is stated that all hopes of the Dundee clipper *Strathmore* are
now abandoned,' said the *Birmingham Post* on 13 October. 'It is
understood that when she left the Thames she carried no less
than 20 tons of gunpowder and spirits as part of her cargo, and it

is feared that fire has broken out on board, and that an explosion with most disastrous consequences followed.'

There was also conjecture of iceberg collision, but the idea of a fire was supported by the bad reputation of the crew (letters from passengers reporting drunkenness and cargo theft had reached England in June), and seemed confirmed by another piece of news — on 11 November, the *Belfast Newsletter* quoted an item from the *Shipping Gazette*.

> 'The *Elise*, *Captain Wallis ... reports that on August 30 ... she passed the hull of a large iron ship abandoned. It appeared to have been recently burnt. At the bow was a man figurehead, painted white ...'*
>
> *There is a general concurrence of opinion in Dundee to the effect that the above applied to the* Strathmore, *and the builders, Messrs Brown and Simpson, feel confident that the* Strathmore *is the vessel referred to. She had a man as a figurehead, and it was painted white ... Messrs Brown and Simpson think that the vessel must have blown up, and that in all probability both passengers and crew perished.*

Back on Grande Île, the survivors knew their friends and families must be gravely worried.

'We ... would often conjecture what our friends at home were doing,' wrote Harold Turner, 'and wonder whether they had given us up as lost ...'

'I felt so sorely for you,' Fanny wrote to her daughter, Fanny Rosamund, 'not knowing what had become of us.'

Fanny senior found some comfort in the thought that prayers would be said for them. 'Frank Carmichael, one of the apprentices, and I were wondering whether any masses were being said for us on All Souls' Day.'

Writing to her daughter later, she told her how much she was missed.

The men knew I had a daughter, but I had never said what like you were [sic]. Mike [O'Riordan] dreamt of you, and to my amazement gave me an exact description of you — hair a shade lighter than mine — even to your rapid walk and short steps ...

I was always afraid of building castles in the air about seeing you again. I scarcely dared think of you ...

I am thankful I was not at home, the suspense would have driven me crazy.

While Fanny was longing for her daughter, Fanny Rosamund believed her mother and brother were dead. She and her husband sought legal advice regarding the settlement of Fanny's and Charlie's estates. The lawyer they consulted had clearly been reading the papers:

On the evidence before me, I can see no room for hope that any of the passengers of the Strathmore *have survived ... It is confirmed that she must have been burnt and the fact that the crew had broached the cargo — probably consisting of spirits — gives this some probability. If such a fire did take place under the carelessness of a disorderly crew, the consequences are only too certainly proved as the vessel also carried some 20 barrels of gunpowder and would be blown up to pieces with all her company.*

Nonetheless, he thought it worth waiting a while before settling matters: '... in view of the possibility that they may have reached one of the less frequented islands of the Pacific, I would suggest that the Estate should not be divided until the elapse of one year from the time the vessel was last heard of.'

Far from the Pacific, way down in the southern Indian Ocean, Fanny and Charlie kept waiting for a ship.

All more or less grieved

In early December another ship passed the island without stopping to rescue the survivors, as Peters' journal reports.

> *8 December begins with fine weather, but towards mid-day the wind freshened from the northward and westward, accompanied with showers of rain.*
>
> *Between one and two o'clock the look-out discovered a barque on the north side of the island, so close that he could distinctly see her fore and aft stays, and even noticed her mainstaysail stopped up the stay, as if to keep it clear of the galley funnel.*
>
> *The look-out, with the assistance of another, soon had a counterpane flying from the flagstaff, and the most of us were so sure that this one would relieve us that they began packing up the few curiosities, ready to take down to the boat when she landed; but what was their disappointment when she stood on without taking the least notice of us.*

'We did our utmost to attract their attention,' wrote Harold Turner, 'but without success.'

'This one makes the third vessel we have sighted since we were thrown ashore here,' added Peters, 'which is now more than five months ago, during which time we have kept a sharp look-out from daylight until dark.'

Some time in those five and a half months after the shipwreck, Wattie Walker turned three. None of the survivors' accounts make any mention of his birthday.

No doubt those long cold months on the island changed all the survivors. They grew thin and dirty, pale and fair-haired, lost fingers and toes to frostbite. They developed enmities, alliances and preoccupations, a new island-bound language. Even their dreams were different.

But if the adults were altered, Wattie became another kind of being.

Within a few months, according to one third-class passenger, the little boy's limbs were 'quite deformed' from lack of exercise. The expression on his face was 'painful to contemplate', and his skin had 'the rigid lines and parchment hue peculiar to that of an old man'.

At two and a half, Wattie had been clean and soft-skinned, active and talkative, every month enlarging his vocabulary, his dexterity with small objects, his capacity to think, to speak clearly, to form sentences, to climb and run and keep his balance. His social, physical and intellectual powers had grown stronger week by week.

On Grande Île, all of this went into reverse. He stopped talking and lost all his new words, his vocabulary swiftly reducing to 'oop' — that one mispronounced word for soup. He regressed physically, rarely moving, unable to feed himself, his small limbs curling up into their prenatal posture, his formerly robust muscles wasting away. His world shrank down to a few square centimetres of damp, filthy blanket and slushy grass over hard stones, to the drinking of soup on Yankee Bill's lap, and the trip outside to defecate, carried there and back in his father's arms. His life had become cold and dirt and hunger, pain and grief and fear.

This backwards progression must have been disturbing to watch — a cruel parody of human existence, a lifespan travelling direct from infancy to old age, gutted of childhood, youth and middle years.

•

Christmas came, and still no ship had rescued the survivors.

'Christmas-day was very cold,' wrote Charlie, 'though midsummer, with snow-squalls — in fact, at home you would have called it seasonable weather.'

'Today being Christmas,' reported Peters in his journal, 'we kept it so far as doing no work goes to keeping it, but we had no wine and cake, &c.'

Fanny was perhaps the only one of the survivors to receive a present: 'On Christmas day Harold brought me three eggs out of five that he had buried for himself when the eggs were plentiful. I shall not forget such a generous action.'

Harold himself modestly omits this event in his own account of the holiday: 'Christmas Day! How all our thoughts turned to former days and to our homes! Long, long ago must our friends have given us up for lost; and no doubt their hearts that day yearned for their lost ones.'

There is no record of Wattie's Christmas morning.

By noon, he was dead.

'About midday,' wrote Peters, 'we were all more or less grieved by the death of Mr Walker's child. He had been ailing for months past, more for the want of proper nourishment than from any other complaint; for if he had not a very strong constitution he never would have survived so long as he did.'

Fanny was perhaps among those 'less grieved', having seen nothing of Wattie during the last months of his life. Still, it was gloomy news: 'Any cheering feelings the season may have brought us were damped by the death of poor little Wattie, who absolutely shrank away to nothing before he died. Poor wee man …'

Harold Turner had never seen much of Wattie, having lived in Black Jack's camp since landing on the island. Like Peters, he was impressed by the strength of Wattie's constitution. He wrote his account three years later, by which time he'd forgotten the child's name: 'On Christmas Day, the little baby-boy, Willie Walker, died; it was, indeed, singular how he survived for so long a time ... I am sure it was a great mercy that it did die, for its life would ever have been a misery to it.'

Did Harold mean that Wattie, even if he had lived, would never have fully recovered his health? Perhaps. More likely he simply thought the child's death was inevitable, and therefore merciful when it finally arrived.

Charlie's account gives the clearest picture of Wattie at the time of his death: 'Poor little Wattie died on Christmas-day at twelve o'clock noon, and was buried next morning. You could almost have blown him away, he was so thin and wasted. He was between three and four years old, I think, and looked like an old man of seventy. His shoulders were up to his ears, and his knees up to his chin, being drawn up that shape by the cold.'

No-one described how the little boy died. Did they know he was dying? Were they watching when he breathed his last breath? Was it a loud rattling breath or a quiet sigh? Was he in the arms of his father, or of Yankee Bill, or was he lying on his blanket with no-one touching him?

Did any of the survivors feel they could have done more to keep Wattie alive? Given him more affection, exercised his limbs, or varied his diet of soup with special invalid meals like the fried birds' brains Charlie devised to sustain Fanny?

Several survivors asserted that all the sick were well looked after. Able seaman Charles Tookey said that 'all the lives were saved that could have been ... all was done for those who died on the island'. The first-class passenger Hilton Keith agreed: '... everything was done for all of them that could be done under the circumstances'. And according to the second steward, David Wilson, who'd cared for old William Husband before his death,

'On the island there was very little to be done for the people who died. There was no neglect ...'

They buried Wattie on Boxing Day.

'We dug a nice little grave for him close by where Mr Henderson was laid,' wrote Peters, 'and buried him the day after he died, reading a chapter out of the Bible over his grave.'

Alfred Walker was there, and so was Yankee Bill. They stood around the tiny grave with the other survivors, 'more or less grieved', their ragged clothes flapping in the freezing wind. Seabirds screamed overhead as the men threw dirt over Wattie's body.

In case of dire necessity

Wattie's death intensified the survivors' longing for home.

'We were all getting very anxious to be off,' wrote Charlie,

> *another winter on the island would, I fear, have left very few to tell the tale, though we were storing skins to burn, and oil also, in case of such a dire necessity.*
>
> *There would have been little to eat. The young albatross were on the island when we landed in July; and ... [now] the old birds [had] returned and built their nests and laid their eggs, so we presumed we had seen the round of the sea-birds.*

The albatrosses had reappeared in November. As the survivors had enough penguins, muttonbirds and mollymawks to eat at the time, they regarded the albatrosses as a kind of winter insurance.

'The old albatross are beginning to land for the purpose of pairing,' reported Peters on 20 November, 'so we have made a law not to kill them, but to leave them alone at present, as there are other kinds of birds which will soon be leaving the island, whereas the albatross will remain on it all winter, so we intend to keep them for our winter stock.'

'We never took any albatross-eggs,' wrote Charlie,

as we looked forward to depending on the young for food later on …

We used to see them, when pairing, bending and bowing to each other like courtiers in the olden time dancing a minuet; but their voices were not equal to their appearance, sounding like a bad imitation of a donkey braying.

At one time, when they were sitting on their eggs, we had, I daresay, about a couple of hundreds or more of the beautiful creatures scattered over the grassy parts of our island. They lay but one egg, and it is scarcely so large as you might expect from the size of the bird: it is white, with pinkish spots on the broad end.

'Their nests were elevated about a foot above the ground,' added Harold Turner, 'and were composed of the thick roots of grass.'

Despite their fear of another Grande Île winter, by 1876 most of the survivors had accepted that another year's imprisonment was almost inevitable. They knew their hunting had affected the island's bird populations, and dreaded more food shortages. Peters made the best of it in his journal.

1 January 1876. We have now been here six months, during which time we have only seen three vessels, which makes us think we will have to winter here, so we are preparing, as far as we are able to do so, by laying in a stock of penguin skins, and also melting down large quantities of fat, which we … put into birds' bladders or [into the] skins of penguins, taken

*off without cutting them down the breast or back and sewing
them up after they are filled up. We will want the fat either for
eating or burning in the lamps, as the birds will be far scarcer
this winter than they were last; but if we can keep up a good
fire (which we can do with plenty of penguins' skins) we will
always manage to pick up a bird now and again, which won't
come so hard on us, as we are all in a more healthy condition
than we were last winter.*

Peters cannot have been thinking of Fanny when he wrote this
— her condition at the time was far from healthy: 'I had been
very ill again … I thought at last that I was going, for although
the state of matters on the island was better, what we had gone
through had told dreadfully on me.'

After Harold Turner's Christmas present there were no more
of the penguin eggs that had strengthened her.

'All the eggs were done,' wrote Charlie, and my mother was
getting exceedingly weak, for she could not eat the bird-flesh
without it making her very sick, and it was only now and then
she could manage to take a little; she said herself she could not
last another fortnight …'

With no proper food or shelter, not much could be done to
help her. There was, as she recalled,

*a little of the famous 'Red Heart rum', put away for the use of
the sick by Mr Peters, which did me incalculable good.*

*… it was such a long time of suffering and endurance … I
was very near death several times, had it not been for Charlie's
constant care and tenderness I should really have gone … Such
tender care he took of me too, never making a fuss about what
he did!*

… I felt I could not last long.

Almost a month after the last ship had passed without seeing them, the survivors decided to improve their signalling system, as Peters reported in his journal.

> *3 January. As two of the ships that passed last came so close to the island and took no notice of our flag, we started today to build a square tower of turf, which is for two purposes — firstly to attract a passing ship's attention; and secondly, to be a sort of shelter for the look-out, as there would always be a lee side to it, where he would not be so much exposed to the inclemency of the weather.*
>
> *We intend to build it high as we can, so that it will show all the farther out to sea, and we also intend to plant a short flagstaff on the top of it, which we will get off our principal flagstaff, where we have it now rigged as a topmast.*
>
> *The digging of the turf is the worst job of all, as we have nothing to dig with except our fingers, our clubs being nearly all used up for killing penguins …*
>
> *Since this year commenced we have had a great deal of foggy weather, which we don't look upon with very favourable eyes, as some of us seem to think that a man-of-war ought to be coming round this way soon, for it seems strange that so many of them are cruising about the world and that none of them should come and take a look at the Crozet Islands once in a while, especially as they lie right in the track of ships bound for the Empire's Colonies.*

Eleven days later, on Friday, 14 January, another ship was sighted.

> *This morning we were startled very early by the look-out singing out 'Sail oh'. The look-out had just gone on the hill at daybreak*

when he discovered a barque under all plain sail standing to the eastward.

Before many minutes had elapsed he had a blanket flying from the flagstaff, besides the small flag which was always flying there in moderate weather, also a couple of hands on the uncompleted monument waving a blanket ...

Harold Turner was sure that the ship 'must have seen our "Turf Tower", which was about twelve feet high, with an oar stuck in the middle and a blanket attached to the top. They seemed quite close to us, and were becalmed. The air was so clear that we could see distinctly for quite thirty miles.'

But if the ship did see the tower, she did not stop to investigate. As Peters wrote: '... the barque sailed away, as the former ones had done, without taking heed of either [flag], leaving us standing straining our eyes looking for the slightest sign of our signal being seen'.

It was the fourth ship that had passed them without stopping.

'As the vessel gradually disappeared from our sight,' recalled Harold Turner, 'we became thoroughly disheartened. All our hope of being rescued seemed to vanish ...'

The happiest day we shall ever know on earth

Within a few days of the ship's passing, the survivors' dashed hopes had revived enough to continue work on their signals, as Peters reported on Tuesday and Wednesday of the following week.

18 January. Some of us being on the hill together, we went and drew up our flagstaff out of the ground, which we did with great difficulty, and we found that it had imperceptibly sunk into the ground about three feet. We struck it into the ground about twenty feet farther to the northward, where we imagined it would show better, as most of the ships passed on that side, only one having passed on the south side.

19 January. As the weather has been very unfavourable these last few days for building purposes, the ground being saturated with rain, we have been unable to work at the tower again until today, when we went to work and built more on it.

When we left off today the tower was about fourteen feet six inches square and between nine and ten feet high, and as it is built solid it takes a great quantity of turf to raise it a few feet; but if the weather keeps favourable we will persevere and get it up [to] the height we want it, which is fixed to be at least twenty-six feet.

The rain came again and did not stop until the Friday, when, as Peters wrote: 'Today commenced with fine weather but the continued building of the tower could not be gone on with on account of the ground being in such a wet condition.'

In the early hours of that fine Friday morning, Fanny dreamed of rescue: 'I awoke quite cheerful and bright, saying, "Charlie, I've seen the ship," (we never dreamt of any but the one that was to take us off).'

Later in the day, the ship came.

'There was not much wind,' wrote Charlie,

and the day was fine. I thought I would give myself a holiday from skinning, so I had just got a 'pig' full of young penguin's legs, and had hung them on a string on the roof to dry and smoke a little, and was backing out of the shanty, when, just visible, I saw a ship.

I yelled out 'Sail ho!' and ran to see if the lookout had seen it from the flag-staff. They had seen her a short time before, and the flags and everything were up; fires were lit also on different parts of the hill so that they might see the smoke, and blankets were about in every position that looked eligible.

Of course we were all very much excited, hope and fear alternately predominating. I had gone to the flag-staff, and was running back to tell my mother not to be too sanguine, as the ship had not as yet altered her course ...

'The vessel seemed to take no heed of our signals,' recalled Peters, 'until she was right abreast of the flagstaff, when she hauled to the wind and headed towards the rock, making the most of us jump about like a lot of lunatics.'

According to the third mate: 'The [ship's] captain, as I hear, had gone up aloft to have a look at the islands, and noticed something unusual, and was standing in to see what it was when the look-out in the crow's nest reported that he saw our signals.'

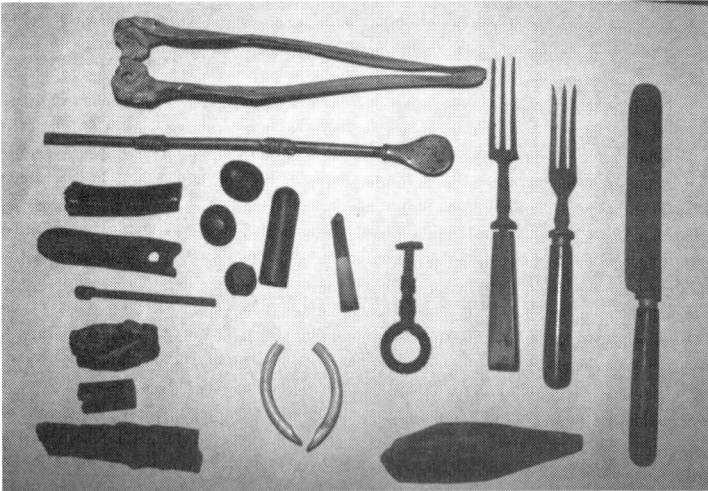

Souvenirs of Grande Île, handed down to Charlie's great-granddaughter Pru FitzHerbert

'[T]his time, thank God,' wrote Harold, '[our signals were] not in vain, for we were seen; and very soon we could see them bearing towards the island ... How to show our joy we could not tell. Some turned somersaults, others turned cart-wheel on their hands, whilst others ran up and down like so many wild beasts.'

Hurrying back down the hill to Fanny, Charlie heard the men's cries, and stopped to look out to sea. 'There — delightful sight! — she had seen us, and was steering close in to the island. Some of us cried with joy ... [It was] the 21st of January 1876, the happiest day we shall ever know on earth ...'

Down at Penguin Cottage, Fanny had also seen the ship change course: 'I sank on my knees at the entrance, and wept tears of joy.'

'When about half a mile off,' recalled Harold, '[the ship] hoisted her ensign, the Stars and Stripes. No one can imagine what was felt at that moment.'

'I packed up all our valuables,' wrote Charlie, 'my club ... knife, fork, and two spoons — and prepared everything for embarking.'

He also, according to Fanny, stripped some of his clothes off, giving her,

> one or two articles of his apparel ... for my wardrobe was reduced to a flannel shirt and petticoat much the worse for wear, and (what I considered very grand) the polonaise you bought me — everything as well as myself black, [and] greasy ... though we did not notice it at that time ...
>
> All made themselves as respectable as they could while as for myself I was ashamed to be seen by a stranger — I was ... dirty and smelt horribly fishy & as the quickest bath possible Charlie cut a penguin's throat over my head & shoulders & shampooed me with the blood ...
>
> What moments of delight were these!

While Fanny and Charlie were hurrying to get ready, the ship was sailing closer, as Peters described: 'As soon as she came about one mile to the eastward of the island she backed her main yards and lowered two boats, to our intense delight … They pulled to the north side of the island, thinking to get a landing there, but they found it was impossible to effect it.'

'We soon saw that she was a whaler from the shape of her boats,' wrote Fanny. 'Unfortunately they came to the wrong side of the island to a place that looked like a good landing place but was not.'

The boats, as Harold Turner wrote, 'came towards us, and we descended to the lower cliffs and onto the rocky beach to meet them. They were unable to come alongside the island, on account of the high wind which was blowing at that time.'

'Those in the boats could not see our signals,' explained Fanny, 'or hear our voices … '

'Our sailmaker stripped,' wrote Harold Turner, 'and, having swam to them, was taken in.'

'"Sails",' added Fanny, 'boldly swam out through the heavy surf & tangled sea weed — a feat of no little danger …'

'We therefore relieved our feelings,' Harold wrote, 'by shouting three cheers in good old English style.'

'As soon as they got him aboard,' reported Peters, 'they pulled round to the other side of the island, where we had first landed …'

There was some confusion, as Fanny described: 'Great was the excitement every where … We first hurried to one side of the island, then to another, scrambling over rocks, holes, and slime — no easy matter. At last we arrived at our old landing-place.'

According to Peters' journal, it seemed at first that the boats would not take any of the survivors immediately: '… as it was fast getting dark the captain, who was in one of the boats, told us

he would be unable to take any of us off that night, but directly
he knew that there was a lady amongst us he brought his boat as
close as he could safely, and got Mrs Wordsworth aboard …'

Sails jumped ashore with a rope to help her on.

'I could get down to a certain part of the rock in safety,'
Fanny wrote, 'but from there I had to be lowered into the boat
… I made my descent as I had my ascent in a "bowline" … To
the uninitiated this bowline looks a very carelessly-made knot,
but it is strong notwithstanding …'

Getting into the boat was a frightening experience for Fanny.

> … the last thing I clung to on the island was … [Sails'] smooth
> fat neck …
>
> as I was being lowered I heard … [him] cry out, 'Don't
> scrape her, rather throw her into the sea.' … Poor 'Sails' was
> ready to jump in for me, being half stripped … but I weakly
> expostulated that I preferred being scraped. For a moment I
> swung in thin air & as the boat rose on the swell I was caught
> … by Captain Gifford and safely placed in the stern …
>
> Captain Gifford [later] congratulated me on my fortitude.
> He said some men had to be helped, and would scarcely come
> at all.

The boat took five more passengers that night: Sails, Charlie,
Peters and two invalids, including John Nicoll, or 'Steam' — the
engineer who'd been spitting blood.

Left behind on the rocks, Black Jack and the rest of the men
watched the boats row away.

'No more could be taken off,' lamented Harold Turner, 'as it
was too dark …'

Fanny, meanwhile, was becoming reacquainted with the
motion of a boat. 'Long before we reached the ship,' she wrote,

'I was sick, of course. Captain Gifford insisted on my staying in the boat, and it was hoisted up with me on board.'

The ship was, in Charlie's words, 'the gallant little bark *Young Phoenix*, American whaler', under the command of Captain Gifford from New Bedford, Massachusetts. Gifford was sailing with his wife Eleanor, or Nellie. She was the only woman on board and, as Fanny explained, she greatly missed female company: 'Her request to her husband as he started for the island was, "Bring me a woman."'

Mrs Gifford was the first woman Fanny had seen since the night of the wreck:

> *I saw a woman — a real live woman ... leaning over the ship's side with a kerchief round her head and a tender sad look in her eyes — Suddenly it struck me where I had seen the face before: it was the fair sweet face of my vision on the island ...*

Nellie, wife of Captain Gifford of the Young Phoenix

I was taken downstairs ... by an 'angel', as she seemed to me, with such a fair tender face — a tall, slender woman, like a lily, in her fresh cotton gown.

She took me dirty, wretched, sick, in her arms, and immediately got a tub of water to wash me, for I could do nothing, I was so ill and weak. She washed, clothed, and fed me with the tenderest gentleness. The best of everything was given me. A bed was arranged on a sofa, with pillows, sheets, and blankets.

For seven months I had thought it a luxury to get a flat stone to sit on, and had hardly ever lain down without my feet in a pool of water; and now, surrounded by every comfort, I did not speak or think, but could only lie and wonder, and thank Almighty God for His mercy ...

It is almost worth being shipwrecked to experience so much kindness.

'It was fortunate for Mrs Wordsworth that the captain's wife was aboard,' commented Harold Turner. 'I am afraid she would have come off badly in the petticoat line had she not been.'

The five men were also well looked after, as Peters wrote: 'As soon as we arrived on board we were received with every possible kindness, being supplied with food and new clothes from head to heel, which, as soon as we had washed ourselves with plenty of warm water, we put on, retiring to rest soon after ...'

'[E]veryone was exceedingly kind to us,' added Charlie.

I don't know how my mother could have managed without ... Captain Gifford's young wife, a most gentle, kind lady ... [My mother] was comfortably cushioned up on a large sofa in the stern cabin; a nicely done up little place, with pictures, books, and harmonium ...

[The Young Phoenix] *was but a small vessel, and had a crew
of 30 hands, so that there was little room to spare, and Mr
Peters and I slept on the floor.*

They did not get much rest, according to Peters, being 'unable to
sleep for thinking of our good fortune, which we could scarcely
realise'.

Back on the island, Black Jack and the other men had been given
supplies.

'They brought us beef and bread,' said the third mate.

'The first moment that Captain Gifford saw distressed people
on the island,' wrote Fanny, 'rightly judging they could not all be
got off the rock that night, he had thoughtfully provisioned the
boats, even to tobacco.'

'[T]hey left us a bag of biscuits and some salt pork,' recalled
Harold Turner, 'both of which we ate with a good relish. After
they left us, we went to our old quarters for the last time. We
slept but little that night, but sat up singing, smoking, and telling
yarns.' Their late night did not make them sleep in, however:
'We were up on the top of the hill before daybreak the next
morning.'

For a short while, the men did not know whether there
was room for them in the *Young Phoenix*, as Charlie explained:
'Captain Gifford was undecided whether he could take us all or
not; however, he made up his mind to manage us as well as he
could, leaving his fishing-grounds — which would be a great loss
to him — and take us to Mauritius or the Cape, unless he could
tranship us to English ships.'

According to the third mate, Gifford considered moving
some of the survivors to Hog Island, to wait until a ship could
be sent to collect them: 'The captain had wished to leave us on

Hog Island until he had finished his cruise ... We should have done well enough on Hog Island. It was a sealing station, and there are pigs and rabbits, and a hut and boiler there.'

Black Jack and his mates did not like this idea. Like all the survivors, they no doubt wanted to get off the Crozets as soon as they could. But the third mate thought they were motivated by fear of arrest for their misconduct on the *Strathmore* — 'the crew would not have it, thinking, as I believe, that he would put into port to land us and they would have a chance of bolting'. Presumably the sailors would have more trouble escaping if the authorities got warning of their whereabouts before they were rescued.

Captain Gifford took pity on them, as Peters reported: 'Captain Gifford, after consultations with his officers, determined to give up his cruise there for the season at a very great sacrifice to their owners, themselves, and their crew; for, by their carrying us to a port they will lose a whole season's fishing, which I have been told amounts on average to from four thousand to five thousand pounds sterling.'

Captain Gifford of the Young Phoenix

The next day, Saturday, 22 January, was exactly four weeks since Wattie's death.

'Poor wee man,' wrote Fanny, 'if he could have held out a little longer he might have been saved ...'

'The day was lovely,' recalled Charlie, 'and we steered for the island again ...'

'As soon as the ship was conveniently placed,' wrote Peters,

three boats were lowered and sent ashore, in the latter of which I went, taking with me four wooden crosses to mark the graves of our four less fortunate companions — placing a bottle, in which was put a short account of our wreck and hardships, also the names and ages, with the dates of death, of those lying under the crosses, beneath the first or lower cross, the neck being left to stick out of the ground, so that if anyone does ever land there they can find out what the crosses represent. The reason why five crosses were not taken ashore was because the first one that died was buried in the sea ...

'The three boats returned three times to take us off,' wrote Harold Turner.

We descended by means of a rope fasted to a piece of projecting rock, and so slipped down into the boats beneath.

On our boarding the vessel, we found the boilers full of hot water for our use. We were certainly in a condition to be washed, for we were filthily dirty. Our clothes, too, skins, and the remnants of the wreck were quite fit to be cast on one side. Clothes were given to us, which we put on after a good washing. We felt like new creatures when we sat down to a capital meal of potatoes and salt meat, with new clothes on, and clean skin. Comfortable quarters were given us between decks, with a sail to cover us.

'The remainder of the crew and passengers,' added Peters, 'were all … treated with the same kindness we had received — forty-three of us being all provided with new under and over shirts, drawers, trousers, shoes, and stockings, and most of us with warm coats and caps, these things being taken out of the ship's outfit for the cruise.'

Sailing north in the *Young Phoenix*, Fanny, Charlie, Black Jack and the other survivors stood on deck in their new clothes, watching Grande Île retreat into the distance: '… we had a capital opportunity of seeing the remainder of the Crozet group,' wrote Harold Turner, 'or Twelve Apostles, as the islands were called. The one we were on was by far the largest.'

None of them owned much more than what they stood up in.

'With the exception of two rings and … [my] rosary,' wrote Fanny to her daughter a few weeks later,

> *I have not a relic of my past life.*
>
> *Even when I thought I was going to the bottom, I regretted our lovely picture of your dear father (a life-size painting of my husband when a boy, with his favourite pony — the figure by Sir Henry Raeburn, and the animal by Howe).*
>
> *However, we have ourselves, and it has been Almighty God's will that we should lose the rest.*

6

After

On leaving the Crozet Islands, Captain Gifford sailed north, planning to land the *Strathmore* survivors on the island of Mauritius, about three thousand kilometres away. But just four days later, on 26 January, when the *Young Phoenix* had travelled less than four hundred kilometres, she met first the Karachi-bound *Sierra Morena*, and then the *Childers*, bound for Rangoon. These two ships between them took all forty-four survivors on the same day, leaving the *Young Phoenix* to resume whale-hunting — the ship would catch about five hundred whales during her two-year voyage.

Captain Gifford, his wife and the crew of the *Young Phoenix* later received various rewards for rescuing the *Strathmore* survivors — medals, watches, sums of money, a pearl ring, a silver claret jug. The presents were given to them by the Dundee Clipper Line, the people of Mauritius, the Shaw Savill & Co shipping agents, the British and New Zealand governments and the survivors themselves.

The good ship *Sierra Morena* took the *Strathmore*'s officers, half her first-class passengers and the whole of third class. The group included second mate Peters, Sails the sailmaker, and the religiously inclined Wilson brothers — 21-year-old David

Wilson, the invalid second steward, and eighteen-year-old Robert Aitkenhead Wilson, whose diary, it seems, was burned by Black Jack.

Black Jack himself transhipped to the *Childers*, along with Yankee Bill, apprentice Harold Turner and almost all the remaining crew, plus the other half of the first-class passengers, including Fanny, Charlie, and Wattie Walker's father, Alfred.

Both ships sailed north, taking the survivors across the equator and up to South Asia. In late February, the *Sierra Morena* reached Point de Galle in Ceylon, now Sri Lanka. After sailing for almost two months on the *Childers*, Fanny, Charlie, Black Jack, Alfred Walker and the rest landed in Rangoon, then the capital of British Burma. From these ports, the survivors dispersed, shipping for Britain, Australia, New Zealand and ports unknown.

Anything to do with the wreck of the *Strathmore* was international news during 1876 and 1877. The testimonials of passengers and crew appeared in the London *Times*, the Wordsworths published their stories in *Blackwood's Edinburgh Magazine*, and the second mate's journal ran in the *Dundee Chronicle*. All were widely reprinted throughout the English-speaking world. In 1878, Harold Turner published a pamphlet on his experiences, which sold for ninepence. Even in later years the story was periodically revisited — the *Auckland Star* ran three feature articles on the wreck as late as 1927.

Much of the 1876 coverage focused on the British Board of Trade inquiry held in early May. Proceedings were conducted at the Greenwich Police Court, where witnesses answered questions about the ship's compasses and cargo, the events of the voyage, the wreck and the months spent on Grande Île. Second mate Peters was the principal witness, and a number of the *Strathmore*'s officers, seamen and passengers also appeared before the court.

The inquiry concluded that the wreck was caused by: '... the imprudence ... of the master in proceeding at night in a dense fog when his dead reckoning showed him that he was in the vicinity of the Crozet Islands, especially as he had had no sights for at least three or four days previously and might have been warned of his proximity to land by passing a quantity of seaweed on the afternoon ... before the disaster.'

The inquiry's report also said the lifeboats should have been better stowed, and praised Captain Gifford of the *Young Phoenix* for his 'noble and generous conduct'. In September, Peters received a Board of Trade medal 'for gallantry in saving life at sea'.

In the months immediately following the rescue, and before the Board of Trade inquiry was held, the personal tragedies of the *Strathmore* were reported in newspapers in Britain and around the world.

In an early London *Times* article, on 28 February, Wattie Walker appeared after his mother, Alice, in the 'List of Passengers Lost — Chief Cabin' as 'Walter A. H. Walker'. On 27 March, he was identified in the paper as 'a little child', one of 'five deaths on the island'. Two days later his was the first name listed under 'Died on the Island': 'W. Walker (a child), first class'. On 9 April, the *New York Times* referred to Wattie as 'a little child, [who died on] Christmas Day', and on the twenty-ninth he was mentioned in the *New Zealand Mail* as a 'little boy [who] died for want of proper nourishment'.

In the newspapers, as in most of the survivors' accounts, Wattie is little more than a tragic footnote. How was he remembered by those who knew him?

The Victorians were sentimental about death, especially the deaths of children. The middle- and upper-class dead were honoured with elaborate funerals, decorative tombstones, black-edged writing paper and dark mourning clothes. Jewellery was made from locks of loved ones' hair: 'Hair is at once the most delicate and lasting of our materials, and survives us, like love,' as *Godey's Lady's Book* put it in May 1855.

Photographs of dead bodies were also popular, particularly photos of dead children, as often no other image of a child existed, since infants frequently died before there was a chance to paint or photograph them.

But of course none of these rituals could be kept in the Crozet Islands. Wattie had no funeral to speak of, no tombstone, no post-mortem photograph. Did his father save a lock of hair from his head to be put into a locket or brooch? Did he write about his son in letters to relatives and friends? Were poems composed in Wattie's honour?

Charlie Wordsworth's *Blackwood's Edinburgh Magazine* article called Wattie 'the last of the unfortunate few whom it was our sad task to bury on that bleak, lonely island'. In the article, Charlie tried his hand at writing a group epitaph for those interred on Grande Île.

Poor fellows! Though their graves lie far from all sounds of human toil, and only the dash of the waves or the sea-bird's cry is heard above their last resting-place; though no stone stands to bear the record of their virtues, and no affectionate hand marks the spot with the humble tribute of flowers — still they will not be forgotten.

In some quiet hour their comrades' thoughts will turn to those lonely graves, far in the midst of the restless ocean, and

surely their hearts will soften with some thought of pity or
regret when they recall the existence there so miserably closed.

How was Wattie remembered within his own family? Was he the
subject of stories told by grandparents, aunts, uncles or cousins
in later years? We know nothing of Wattie's extended family and
almost nothing of his father's later life.

Fanny Wordsworth mentioned Alfred Walker in a cheerful
moment on board the *Childers*, when it was moored near
Rangoon.

Charlie and Mr Walker sleep on the two couches in the saloon…
and last night when they came down to go to bed, to their
astonishment they found two long dark figures [local stevedores]
stretched out in their places, so all they could do was to have a
hearty laugh, and sleep on the floor.

According to Ian Church's book *Survival on the Crozets*, Alfred
Walker settled in New Zealand, where he 'became a well-known
Auckland sharebroker and an enthusiastic bowler'. Apparently
he died at the age of eighty-four, on 30 June 1926, fifty-one years
less a day after the wreck of the *Strathmore*.

The Crozets are not much visited — there is a research
station on Île de la Possession, but the Twelve Apostles still
belong to the penguins and albatrosses. As far as I know,
Wattie's bones remain on Grande Île. Perhaps his name,
age and date of death are still legible inside the bottle that
the second mate buried nearby — though, as Peters left the
bottleneck above ground, probably not. Over a hundred years
of relentless rain and wind have no doubt flattened out the
mound of earth over Wattie's grave, and destroyed the wooden
cross that marked it.

•

The fate of Black Jack Warren and his mates was not recorded in the press. After boarding the *Young Phoenix* on the morning of 22 January, Black Jack and the other survivors of the *Strathmore* crew stripped off to scrub themselves in the hot water from the ship's boilers.

If Jack's black frockcoat was not too far gone, he may have washed it as well as himself, rather than accept a coat from the ship's stores — there were not coats and caps enough to go round. He was issued with a new shirt, however, plus trousers, underclothes, shoes and stockings.

Once clean, the men were served their meal of salt pork and potatoes, which made some of them ill, after six months of living on seabirds.

For the next four nights, Jack and his mates slept 'tween decks, under a sail. It was cold, especially for those with no coats, and there were cockroaches, but it was far warmer and dryer than Black Jack's shanty, with its stone floor and the tendency of the front wall to collapse.

Perhaps they lent the *Young Phoenix* crew a hand, but the *Strathmore* men were not put on watches. There were sailors enough to work the *Young Phoenix* — she had a large crew for her size, according to Charlie Wordsworth — so Jack got a good rest before transhipping to the *Childers*.

In contrast to the American sailors on the *Phoenix*, the *Childers* crew, as Fanny wrote, were 'all blacks, some rather handsome'. Perhaps they were South-East Asian 'lascars', though as most of them were 'colossal' it is more likely they were Guinea Coast Africans. Both races would have been familiar to Black Jack from his Limehouse days in London, and it seems the two crews were friendly.

'They are a very merry lot,' wrote Fanny of the *Childers* crew, 'and, when work is done, fond of a little music or dancing ... their laugh is worth hearing.'

On the *Childers* there were rats in the sailors' quarters, instead of cockroaches. Probably the ship was larger than the *Young Phoenix*, and perhaps some blankets were found for the *Strathmore* men. Within a few weeks they would not need them, as they sailed out of sub-Antarctic waters into warmer latitudes, heading roughly north-east across the Indian Ocean.

They were soon in the tropics. In March they sighted Sumatra, sailed north into the Andaman Sea — 'calm as a lake', wrote Fanny, 'scarcely a breath of wind' — and up towards the Irawaddy River: 'a most dangerous coast, with sand-banks stretching far out, and the pilots will only come to the mouth of the river, when the worst danger is over ... The currents are so strong that even with a strong breeze the ship cannot keep its own.'

On 15 March, Fanny reported, the *Childers* got into trouble in shallow waters.

> [there was] a great trampling on deck and hurrying about, sails being dragged up and down... I heard the man say, 'Only three fathoms water,' and I at once knew we were within a few inches of being aground ... [and indeed we] slightly grazed the bottom ...
>
> The ship was like a bee-hive, every one was so busy. In a very short time every sail was furled and the anchor dropped ... when [let] go it [went] ... with a vengeance, the huge chain snapping like a bit of wood, and off went the anchor with thirty fathoms of valuable chain cable ... there were five more on board; and another was soon dropped.

Fanny saw Black Jack's mate Old Jack Evans, who'd 'been wrecked five or six times', run laughing across the deck: '"... it would be queer if we were wrecked twice this voyage," he said, "there must be some Jonahs amongst us, I think".'

But the *Childers* passed the danger safely. By Friday, 17 March, she was at the river mouth, where half a dozen ships lay at anchor, and the stevedores — 'turbaned Mussulmans' — came aboard. Next morning the pilot joined them, and a tugboat towed the ship up the river to Rangoon. There were, as Fanny described, 'All sorts of queer boats, Chinese junks, sampans, and barges to be seen as we turned into the narrower parts of the river ... we could just see the dome of the golden pagoda ... a thing like a huge umbrella of pure gold on the top ...' This was the Shwedagon Pagoda, reputedly built during the lifetime of the Buddha, and housing eight hairs from his head.

The *Childers* crew passed a hat around and sent Black Jack and his mates on shore, where they were put up at the Railway Hotel, with one and a half rupees each. They also received another sum of money which, according to Harold Turner, caused some disgruntlement: '... but for the false statement of one of the passengers concerning the conduct of the crew, we should have had divided amongst us the sum of 1000 rupees, which had been promised by the merchants of Rangoon. Instead of that, we only got ten rupees each.'

If this tale is true, which passenger robbed Harold, Black Jack and the others of their extra forty-odd rupees?

Certainly Harold did not mean to accuse Fanny. They clearly liked each other, and she thought him 'a very fine character ... simple, brave and unselfish'. Fanny was deeply grateful to the crew, and Charlie was their 'great favourite' — surely neither he nor his mother maligned the sailors.

So the mystery passenger must have been either the nineteen-year-old Hilton Keith or Wattie's father, Alfred Walker.

Fanny had spoken of receiving help from 'young Mr Keith' during the wreck and its aftermath, and Charlie was friendly with him — the two young men had shared a cabin on the *Strathmore*. But neither Charlie nor Fanny made much mention of Mr Walker, Fanny rather pointedly omitting him when publicly thanking the first-class passengers who'd helped her. Also, perhaps, as an older man, Walker was more likely to criticise others in public.

But to be fair to Walker, Harold Turner was undoubtedly prone to exaggeration, and his story of the thousand rupees has the ring of legend.

This is the last we see of Black Jack — living it up in the Railway Hotel with his new suit of clothes, his eleven and a half rupees. Surely there were a few free drinks for the brave sailors who'd survived the terrible wreck of the good ship *Strathmore*, at least before any rumours of misconduct got abroad. Did the men resent the slur on their reputation, throwing a punch or two in the steamy public bars of Rangoon?

Perhaps Jack bolted even before he got his ten rupees, before the British authorities could arrest him. Pausing only for a night of serious drinking with Old Jack Evans, Funny Lad and Yankee Bill, he slept through his hangover, maybe, before signing on, under a false name, to the crew of some merchant vessel carrying a cargo of rice and timber, cotton and cheroots, ivory and gemstones.

Known to history only through the wreck of the *Strathmore*, Jack's name slipped out of the public record once more, as the man himself sailed off — bound perhaps for the pubs of Shadwell and Limehouse via India, Australia and ports unknown.

•

The story of Charlie Wordsworth has been much more closely chronicled, even outside the histories kept by his own family, perhaps in part due to the three wrecks in his life: the one he survived, the one he narrowly missed and the one that finally killed him.

After their rescue from the Crozet Islands, Charlie and Fanny spent almost a week in Rangoon before departing for Liverpool in late March 1876. They embarked on the steamship *Chancellor*, along with five other *Strathmore* survivors: two sailors and the young apprentices Harold Turner, Ted Preston and Frankie Carmichael.

The *Chancellor* stopped at Aden for coal, then steamed up the Red Sea and the Suez Canal to Port Said, where more coal was loaded. The ship then crossed the Mediterranean, making a last stop at Malta before steaming out into the Atlantic and up to the British Isles.

Charlie and his mother landed at Liverpool on 2 May 1876, more than a year after their departure on the *Strathmore*.

Less than three months after returning to Britain, Charlie was married. Less than six weeks after his wedding, he sailed for New Zealand once again, accompanied this time by his wife.

Charlie's wife, Georgiana, photographed around the time of her marriage

Charlie's bride was twenty-year-old Georgiana Cowan, the orphaned daughter of an Edinburgh physician. Georgiana was a Protestant, but she — along with her older sister Kate — converted to Catholicism before the wedding. At about this time Georgiana was given the *Album to Record Feelings & Thoughts* in which Charlie and Fanny's *Confessions* appear. According to Georgiana's own entry in the book, she shared Charlie's enthusiasm for Sir Walter Scott, and was unable to open her mouth without putting her foot in it. She preferred to live 'Not very far from Edinburgh' — an ambition she was not destined to realise.

The young couple sailed for New Zealand in September 1876, on the *Avalanche*, another Shaw Savill & Co clipper. On the way, according to the *Taranaki Herald*, the *Avalanche* 'visited the Crozet Islands, but obtained no additional information about the wrecked *Strathmore*'. The ship stopped long enough for Charlie to make a sketch of Grande Île.

On 8 December, the *Avalanche* landed Charlie and Georgiana safely in Wellington. It was the ship's last successful colonial voyage — after embarking again for New Zealand just a year later, the *Avalanche* collided with another ship and was wrecked. All her passengers and all but three of her crew were lost.

Less than two weeks after arriving in New Zealand, Charlie was up in Hawke's Bay, in the central North Island. Georgiana, in the early months of pregnancy, remained behind in Wellington. Charlie wrote to her from Napier's Criterion Hotel:

> ... *above all take care of your own dear little self — no lifting heavy things, stooping — or stretching — no matter what anyone says, look after yourself & don't over work or tire yourself. Get yourself a couple of cool dresses if you want them*

but [be careful] with the money ... With this piece of advice I
close my letter & put in it all the love I possibly can.

Charlie wanted to buy land, but first he needed to find at least
a temporary home for his new family. The next day he wrote
again, from a nearby sheep station.

Dearest Dottles ... I rode here this morning from Waipukurau
on a borrowed horse ... I have already got the offer of a place on
a station but shall not decide too hurridly [sic] as it is in very
rough inaccessible country & you might have some difficulty
in getting there, [it] is done on pack horses. It will not be long
before I settle somewhere ...

Write home to my mother by the next mail & tell her of my
doings, I have no time or opportunity to write home letters. Tell
her what a darling you are from me & with love. To her, that
will be my only message.

Within a few months, Charlie had taken up a property at
Kaikora (now Otane), near Waipukurau. The *Hawke's Bay Herald*
announced that he was 'about to settle permanently in Hawke's
Bay', and in May 1877 his and Georgiana's first child was born
there: Winifred Mary.

At Kaikora, Charlie farmed his land, set up as an agent for the
New Zealand Insurance Company and worked for an auctioneer
in nearby Waipawa. But apparently his career in Hawke's Bay was
not as successful as he'd hoped. By the time his next daughter
was born, two and a half years later, the Wordsworths had left
the district for a new property further south — Silverford, near
the town of Ashhurst in the Manawatu.

Charlie's second child, Eleanor Gifford Wordsworth, was
named after the captain's wife on the *Young Phoenix*, though

the family always called her Toddy. A third daughter, my great-grandmother Olive Frances, was born two years later in 1882.

At Silverford, Charlie subscribed to the *New Zealand Tablet* (a Catholic publication), republished his account of the *Strathmore* wreck in an Auckland newspaper, corresponded with the Manawatu Highways Board regarding roads near his property and was taken to court by Chas. Pownall & Co (Scriveners & Mortgage Agents) for having, in the words of the *Evening Post*, 'induced the plaintiffs to raise a loan and then neglected to take advantage of it' — the case was decided in Charlie's favour.

The Manawatu was rough country, only recently settled, and life was not easy. 'My Mother did a brave thing there once,' recalled the Wordsworths' daughter Toddy: '… she was always brave. The dangerous Manawatu River rose in flood … my Father was expected home after dark and would have ridden across the usual ford, there being no other way as the ferry was on our side. The ferry men … refused to take the boat over so my Mother took it herself.'

After five years in the Manawatu district, Charlie sold up again. In September 1884 the family sailed for Australia, where, according to Toddy, Charlie worked on a Sydney newspaper. The

Charlie Wordsworth in the 1880s, 'always good with boats and horses'

Wordsworths' fourth daughter, Zoë, was born in Australia in February 1885, but before she was three months old the family was back in New Zealand, arriving in Auckland on 30 April. Beginning to run out of money, they settled on nearby Waiheke Island.

'We lived on fish and rabbits mostly,' recalled Toddy, 'and once a week rowed out to the cutter which passed, for mail and stores. We left Waiheke by that same cutter and all the crew were drunk. My father locked most of them up and managed — he was always good with boats and horses.'

After nearly two years on Waiheke Island, Charlie got a job in Argentina. The family sailed for South America in February 1887 — two adults and four girls aged from ten to two. They travelled on the *Coptic*, steerage all the way, along with 35,568 frozen sheep.

The new job was on a property about three days journey from Buenos Aires.

'There seemed to be about six large waggons [sic],' wrote Toddy, 'each drawn by eight or ten horses and flocks of horses were driven along with us and were changed into the waggons every now and then. One night we slept in a tremendous wool shed, after that there was nothing but bare horizon.'

The property, remembered by Toddy as Estancia Loma Quen, was an old mission station planted with orchards.

> *There was every kind of beast and bird from flamingoes flying overhead like a pink cloud to the tiniest little humming birds and many with beautiful plumage ... There were bats and hideous toads always hopping about the kitchen floor gobbling up flies ... beautiful ducks about the shores of the lagoon. It was a paradise for us children, but it had its serpent.*

The serpent was the manager of the property, a Mr Kelly.

He was a tremendous man with black hair all over his face …
his great joy, if there was nothing worse to do, was to sting our
bare legs with nettles …

I know both my Mother and Father worked here terribly
hard. I can't bear to think of it … There was only a native
woman to help my Mother … and dear little Bessie was born
here, the fifth little girl …

There came a time when it could be born [sic] no longer and
one hot evening my Mother gathered us into our big room and
we all knelt down and prayed for a long time while my Father
and Mr Kelly fought it out.

The Wordsworths left Argentina after this, travelling steerage to England — 'this time there was no money and we … landed barefooted in London'.

All seven Wordsworths stayed with Mrs Wood, Fanny's well-to-do sister.

'They were good to us,' wrote Toddy, 'and how we loved Aunt Bessie … We children had a donkey and the groom took us gently round the Park … I expect we were very troublesome.'

At some point during their travels the Wordsworths visited Edinburgh, where they stayed with Annie Bisset, Georgiana's stepmother. She offered to keep Toddy and her older sister, Winifred, and pay for their education — 'but that was not agreed to of course,' wrote Toddy later. 'I remember long talks and a lot of weeping.'

Perhaps Annie Bisset helped Charlie with the cost of return passages to New Zealand, where he and Georgiana scraped out a living in the small North Island settlement of Manaia.

'We settled in a poor little four-roomed house in a poor little village in Taranaki,' recalled Toddy, 'and my Father drove the groceries cart and left groceries at the back doors of the people round. The grocer was Mr Cullen and he always made us stand on his counter and be admired by all his customers … My Father worked for the *Hawera Star*, when the spirit moved, and held a night school, but I don't think he was fond of teaching and am sure no one wanted to learn.'

Charlie and Georgiana's son, Gerald — known as Ged — was born at Manaia in 1890. He was named after Georgiana's brother Gerald, who left his sister what Toddy called a 'little fortune' when he died that year.

> *We bought land and built a nice house. It was a small but good bit of land quite near the township and we had some horses and cows and took the milk to the factory like everyone else and we grew up and went to the Public School and were completely wild and naughty — in fact quite notorious.*

Manaia was to be Charlie's home for eight years — longer than he'd lived anywhere since his departure for New Zealand on the *Strathmore*. He became an agent for the Phoenix Fire Assurance Company and took up the local branch of a land agency, advertising frequently in the *Hawera & Normanby Star*.

In Manaia, Charlie's daughters passed school examinations, attended fancy dress balls and won prizes for sewing, running and drawing. Charlie was a member of the Hospital and Charitable Aid Board, the Manaia School Committee, the Manaia Caledonian Society and the Catholic Art Union Committee. He was secretary of the Manaia Hack Racing Club and poundkeeper for the Manaia Town Board.

On Sunday, 29 November 1896, a month after his son's sixth birthday, Charlie took his two eldest girls out fishing on a whaleboat. Winifred was nineteen, Toddy sixteen.

'All went well until about five chains off the shore,' reported the *Egmont Star*, 'when a big sea was seen approaching ...'

The boat capsized, sending its eight passengers into the surf. Winifred, Toddy and three of the men got hold of the upturned hull and soon made it to nearby Waingongoro Beach, but Charlie, along with another man and a young girl, Clara Crowhurst, were washed away from the boat.

'[M]y sister and I found ourselves on the desolate beach,' wrote Toddy, 'between great cruel breakers and sheer cliffs, watching and waiting.'

Onlookers later described the 'blanched faces of the poor girls, who wandered up and down the beach in utter distraction ...'

Over two hours passed before they heard anything of their father — 'at about 2.30,' related the *Egmont Star*,

> *the body of Wordsworth was seen about 100 yards out, tossing about in the breakers ... Deceased was very much bruised ... [and] bore the appearance of having been dashed against the rocks ...*
>
> *Wordsworth, who was perfectly at home in the water, was seen helping Miss Crowhurst, and the actual finding of the bodies seems to indicate that he had nobly sacrificed himself in his endeavour to save her ...*
>
> *It is thought that Mr Wordsworth, who is spoken of as a good swimmer, had hold of Miss Crowhurst all the time, and that when his body was dragged ashore, that of the girl was also brought in, but was pulled from his death grasp when shallow water was reached ... Wordsworth's right hand was closed as if he had grasped something, and the theory is he lost his life trying to save the girl ... His well-known pluck certainly supports such a theory, and his thrilling experience years ago as a castaway had tended to steady his nerves under similar circumstances.*

The paper went on to sum up Charlie's life, getting rather confused between the wrecks of the *Strathmore* and *Avalanche*.

> *Mr Wordsworth, who was a well-known settler on the coast, had a thrilling experience in connection with the wreck of the* Avalanche *... He had ... been wrecked and for two years a castaway in a barren island, where he subsisted along with his mother, and others belonging to the ill-fated* Avalanche, *on birds and their eggs ...*
>
> *Occasionally during his six or eight years residence in this district Mr Wordsworth had been connected with the* Star, *and had contributed not a few thoughtful articles on various subjects. As a genial courteous gentleman he will be mourned by all who knew him ... He was plucky and adventurous, true to his friends, and devoted to his family.*

Twenty years after being rescued from shipwreck by a whaler, Charlie Wordsworth was drowned in the wreck of a whaleboat. He was forty-four years old.

'After [several] hours somebody came and drove us home,' wrote Toddy. 'We ran in to tell my mother but she seemed to know as soon as she saw us.'

Survival is only ever temporary. On returning to England after her rescue, Fanny Wordsworth — the only woman to survive the wreck of the *Strathmore* — had just eight years left to live.

A week after landing in Liverpool, Fanny wrote to *The Times*, thanking second mate Peters and others who had helped her during the wreck and her time on Grande Île. She remained in England for some six weeks, staying with her sister Bessie Wood in Sussex. Before the end of May she had acquired the fashionable new gown in which she had her picture taken at the Robinson &

Cherrill photography studio in Tunbridge Wells. She was still in Sussex in mid June, when she wrote another letter in praise of Peters, this one to the Board of Trade.

By July she was back in Edinburgh, at 2 Forth Street — the address from which Charlie was married at the end of the month.

For the next four years, Fanny lived in Britain, dividing her time between her home in Edinburgh and those of her sister and daughter in England. In the opinion of her Edinburgh friend Elizabeth Dyer, writing to Charlie's wife in December 1880, all this moving around was bad for Fanny's health: '… [she] has been really very poorly, sometimes confined to bed. Dr — did his best for her & soon got her on her feet, but still she requires rest, care, & above all a contented mind, which with one thing & another is not easy for her to obtain, between the Woods, Finlays [family connections in Edinburgh] & Fanny [Rosamond].'

Despite her ill-health, in late 1880 Fanny was going ahead with a second attempt to migrate to New Zealand. She booked a passage to Wellington with Shaw Savill & Co, and once more did the rounds of her goodbyes in Edinburgh. Soon, she was on her way down to London. She spent Christmas in England before boarding the steamer *Norfolk* at the end of January. The voyage, according to the *Star* newspaper in March 1881, was 'an extremely agreeable one, the weather being remarkably mild and pleasant … The monotony of the voyage was relieved by a succession of entertainments. One death took place on Feb. 17 — Emma Young, aged seven years, of croup …'

On arriving in Wellington on 30 March, Fanny sailed immediately for Wanganui — the port closest to the district of Manawatu, where Charlie was living at the time. She brought generous gifts for his family, as his daughter Toddy recalled: 'Grandma Wordsworth came out to us there with cases of clothes made by Worth, even milking dresses, and a piano ... I am glad I remember her so well — carefully and tenderly drying us and brushing our hair and reading to us.'

Apparently Fanny did not move in with her son, and it is unclear whether she settled in the Manawatu. At any rate, two years later, at the end of June 1883, the *Evening Post* reported her arrival in the capital:

> *Most people will remember the wreck of the* Strathmore *upon the Crozets, and the thrilling adventures and hardships of the survivors upon that desolate island. It may be interesting to mention that the lady member of that memorable body of castaways, Mrs Wordsworth, is now in Wellington having arrived by the SS* Ionic, *with the intention, we believe, of taking up her abode here. Mrs Wordsworth, it is satisfactory to learn, is apparently enjoying the best of health, having, it would seem, suffered no permanent injury from the very trying experience which she went through with so much courage and endurance during her sojourn on the island.*

Newspapers often make mistakes. The *Post* had first reported Fanny's arrival in the colony in 1878, over two years before she even left Britain (supposedly she then sailed on the *Strathcathro*, captained by second mate Peters from the *Strathmore*).

It is also highly unlikely that Fanny ever came to Wellington on the steamship *Ionic*, which arrived from London in June 1883. However, she may well have moved down from the Manawatu at this time, and it is possible that her health had improved.

Certainly Fanny was in Wellington by the latter half of 1884. She was living on The Terrace — a long street with harbour views that climbs from the Parliament toward Mount Cook, above the centre of town.

On 15 September 1884, Fanny waved goodbye to her son, daughter-in-law and three granddaughters — they were off to Melbourne in the *Manapouri*. Just a few weeks later, in November, she was ill in bed with what her doctor believed to be meningitis.

On 29 November, at her home on The Terrace, Fanny Wordsworth died. She was buried two days later.

In an article entitled 'The Heroine of the Crozets', the *Star* newspaper, on 1 December, was among the first to report Fanny's death: 'Mrs Frank Wordsworth, known as the heroine of the Crozets, she being the only female who escaped at the wreck of the *Strathmore*, and for many months participated in the hardships and sufferings of the survivors until rescued, died on Saturday evening, aged 58.'

This article was repeated, with minor variations, in the *Taranaki Herald*, the *Hawke's Bay Herald*, the *Bruce Herald*, the *Wanganui Herald*, the *Wanganui Chronicle*, the *Marlborough Express*, the *Feilding Star*, the *Hawera & Normanby Star*, the *Nelson Evening Mail*, the *Tuapeka Times*, the *Southland Times*, the *West Coast Times*, the *Mataura Ensign*, the *Grey River Argus* and the *Otago Witness*. Most of the papers repeated the name 'Mrs Frank Wordsworth', and some called her 'Mrs Francis Wordsworth'. Only the *Hawke's Bay Herald* got her name right.

On 12 December, the *New Zealand Tablet* (a Catholic paper read by both Fanny and Charlie) announced Fanny's death — 'with feelings of deep regret' — describing her as a 'most devout and estimable Catholic lady'.

> *Mrs Wordsworth … was a convert to Catholicity, but it would not require a Catholic reader [of her* Blackwood's *Magazine letter] to tell her faith. She determined that for herself by the various professions of faith appearing in the pages of her story. She says in the first shock of the appalling danger she bethought*

*herself of her rosary and went below to procure it and put it
round her neck.*

According to the *Tablet*, Fanny's 'trials ... on the bleak and
inhospitable Crozet Islands, so graphically described with true
feminine liveliness ... laid the seeds of the decay to which she...
now succumbed'. The *Evening Post* agreed: 'She failed to recover
from the severe shock to the system occasioned by the wreck
and the privations she experienced during the six months she
spent upon the Crozets and had been ailing for a considerable
time prior to her death.'

Perhaps this illness that had plagued Fanny for so long was
of a mild nature, enabling Charlie to feel he could leave her

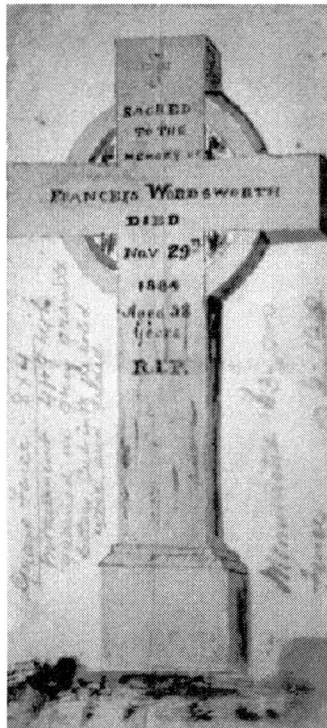

*The initial design for Fanny's
gravestone, sketched by Charlie*

alone in Wellington. And perhaps her poor health did begin on the Crozet Islands — she said herself that her constitution was 'entirely changed'. If so, the 'miracle' of her survival was indeed temporary — it was the wreck of the *Strathmore* that killed her, though it took eight years to finish the job.

Five months after Fanny's death, Charlie Wordsworth left Australia and returned to New Zealand with his family. He had missed his mother's funeral, but he designed a marble memorial and arranged for it to be erected over her grave in Wellington.

A hundred and twenty-four years later, in 2008, I also left my home in Australia and returned to New Zealand, where I enrolled in Wellington's Victoria University to work on this book. Only after a year of walking up The Terrace on my way to campus — wondering which of the big old wooden houses had been Fanny's — did I realise I had been passing within metres of my great-great-great-grandmother's grave.

Fanny is buried near the entrance to the old Mount Street Cemetery, near the university's Student Union building. The gravestone Charlie designed is in fragments now, but some of the words can still be seen.

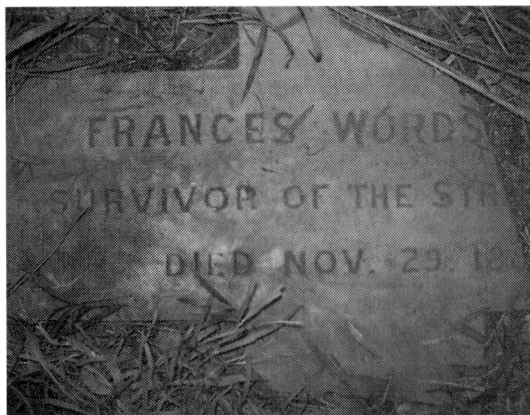

A fragment of Fanny's gravestone

After nearly three years exploring Fanny and Charlie's story, I'm still curious about them. Who were they? Why did they want to emigrate? What were their lives on Grande Île really like? What kept them going when they lost hope? How had they changed by the time of their rescue? There is simply not enough information to answer these questions conclusively. The Wordsworths were ordinary people; for the most part no-one found the evidence of their lives interesting enough to preserve, aside from those documents and artefacts directly relating to the shipwreck. And perhaps my questions would have puzzled even Fanny and Charlie themselves — the truths of a life, if there are such things, may be no easier to discern from inside that life than to uncover over a century later.

For what it's worth, I believe Charlie was affected by his experiences in the Crozet Islands for the rest of his life. The hastiness of his wedding and re-embarkation for New Zealand in the months after his rescue suggest a defiant response to the shipwreck, a determined refusal to be thwarted in his plans. If I'm right, the wreck of the *Strathmore* both shaped the rest of his life and was a root cause of the lives of all his dozens of descendants — including my own.

The apparent restlessness and wanderlust that characterised Charlie's married life may also have owed something to his time on Grande Île — a dislike of feeling stuck in one place, perhaps, or a belief that difficulty is best solved by physical removal. Perhaps, too, the evident strength of his feelings for his children was somehow shadowed by the experience of witnessing Wattie's decline and death on the island. Maybe even the fluctuation of Charlie's financial fortunes can be traced back to the Crozets in some way. A man who expects his projects to fail, who tends to respond to failure by abandoning one ship and jumping aboard another, may well be prone to unwise business decisions.

It is not so easy to find reverberations of the shipwreck in Fanny's later years — but then her age, sex and secure income made her life less eventful, less full of significant choices, than that of a young man with his way to make in the world. She took no sudden actions on her return to Scotland, delaying her re-embarkation for New Zealand for five years. By her own account she became fearful of the sea after surviving the wreck, and her next sea passage was by steamer — a swifter and safer option than sailing. Her reluctance to make another voyage may well have made Charlie more receptive to marrying, as a way of securing female companionship in her absence.

Since Fanny did eventually follow Charlie to New Zealand, perhaps the shipwreck deepened the always strong bond between mother and son — though clearly they were never overly dependent on each other. It may seem melancholy that Charlie was away when Fanny died, though I like to think he left for Australia with his mother's blessing, just as on his earlier New Zealand departures.

Certainly it was sad for his wife and children that Charlie died so early, and just as he seemed to have finally settled down. Perhaps they could admire the heroism that led to his death. I believe he died as he wanted to live — actively, courageously, in the company of his family.

As for my own life, three years in the imaginative company of Charlie and Fanny has helped me move on, emotionally and creatively, from the sense of loss and failure with which I began researching the wreck of the *Strathmore*. My ancestors' story has yielded a radio feature, a Masters thesis and now a book. Soon I'm off to India for a writer's residency in the foothills of the Himalayas, and I recently fell in love. Fanny's and Charlie's courage in the face of shipwreck has helped me be braver, hold less tightly to my plans for the future, open up to the twists and turns of life.

Metric equivalents for imperial measures

1 foot	30.48 centimetres
1 yard	0.91 metres
1 mile	1.61 kilometres
1 pint	0.57 litres
1 gallon	4.55 litres
1 pound	0.45 kilograms
1 ton	1.02 tonnes
	1016 kilograms
1 knot	1.85 kilometres per hour

Sources

In researching this book, I relied where I could on first-hand accounts — the testimony of survivors, preserved through diaries, letters, press archives and books — and on other contemporary records.

These sources are of questionable accuracy — frequently contradicting each other, and often containing details that are puzzling, if not patently incorrect. I have tried to be truthful, but this book is really my best guess at what happened — a likely version of events. For example, all sources agree that the *Strathmore* was wrecked in the early hours of the morning of 1 July 1875, but did the ship strike the rocks at three thirty, three forty-five or four o'clock? I have chosen not to interrupt the story by noting every such case of uncertainty. But in places where the doubt is especially strong, or concerns matters of significance, I have made it clear that I am guessing.

Though I value historical accuracy, in writing this book I was most interested in giving readers a taste of what it was like to live through the wreck of the *Strathmore* and its aftermath. Trusting in the power of story to convey experience, I shaped the raw material of real life — random, inconclusive, messy and poorly recorded as it is — into what I hope is a compelling narrative. I did not contradict the facts, but I often chose to arrange them in the most dramatic sequence, even when I was unsure of the exact order in which they occurred. This process of story-making has inevitably distorted events to some extent. Since I had to choose some way to arrange the material, since no narration — however transparent — can truly arrive at reality, and since even the eyewitnesses of the wreck did not agree on what really happened, I hope my readers will forgive me.

The following list of sources includes only those texts of which I have made substantial use. My background research was both too wide and too shallow to list here; I consulted a very long list of publications, but made use of only small portions of their contents. Any sources from which I quote are either acknowledged within the narrative, or listed here.

Church, Ian, *Survival on the Crozets*, Heritage Press, Waikanae, New Zealand, 1985, includes testimony from Robert Aitkenhead Wilson (TCP), Thomas Henderson (FCP)

Dyer, Elizabeth, Letter to GCW (HBPF), 16 December 1880

Peters, Thomas Brown, Journal: June 1875–January 1876, from a transcript held by his granddaughter Julie Biller (a slightly different version was published widely from 1876)

The Times
    'The *Strathmore*', 29 March 1876, includes testimony from John Allan (third mate), Frederick Bentley (FCP), George Crombie (FCP), John Wilson (AB), Robert Aitkenhead Wilson (TCP)
    'The *Strathmore*', 6 April 1876, includes testimony from Spencer Joslen (FCP), John Pirie (carpenter)

'The *Strathmore*', 3 May 1876, includes testimony from Peter Feathers (compass adjuster), Thomas Peters (second mate)

'The *Strathmore*', 4 May 1876, includes testimony from Allan, Peters

'The *Strathmore*', 5 May 1876, includes testimony from Allan, George Buttenshaw (chief steward), Joslen, Peters, Pirie, John Smith (cook), Walter 'Sails' Smith (sailmaker), John Wilson

'The *Strathmore*', 17 May 1876, includes testimony from Hilton Keith (FCP), Peters, Charles Tookey (AB), second steward David Wilson

Turner, Harold, *The wreck of the Strathmore, or, How we lived on one of the Crozette Islands in the Southern Sea for twenty-nine weeks: a true narrative*, Fleetwood, Lancashire, England, 1878

Wordsworth, Charles Francis
 Letter to FRWB (HBPF), 21 May 1875
 Entry in CARTF (HBPF), c June 1876
 'The Strathmore: Mr Wordsworth's Narrative', *Blackwood's Edinburgh Magazine*, No. DCCXXXI, Vol. CXX, September 1876
 Letter to GCW (HBPF), 21 December 1876
 Letter to GCW (HBPF), 22 December 1876

Wordsworth, Eleanor Gifford 'Toddy', 'Memoir' (HBJG), 15 August 1943

Wordsworth, Frances Young
 Letter to FRWB (HBPF), 21 May 1875
 'A Survivor's Story' (from notebook HBJG), c February 1876
 Letter to FRWB (from notebook HBJG), c 18 February 1876
 Letter to the Editor, dated 9 May, *The Times*, 11 May 1876

Entry in CARTF, c June 1876, (HBPF)

Letter to Board of Trade, dated 18 June, *The Arbroath Guide*, 23 September 1876

'The *Strathmore*: Letter from Mrs Wordsworth, the Lady who Survived the Wreck', *Blackwood's Edinburgh Magazine*, No. DCCXXXI, Vol. CXX, September 1876

Wordsworth, Georgiana Cowan, Entry in CARTF (HBPF), c June 1876

Wordsworth, Larry, 'The Wandering Wordsworths', private publication, 2001

Abbreviations

AB	able seaman
CFW	Wordsworth, Charles Francis
CARTF	*Confessions: An Album to Record Thoughts & Feelings* (GCW's commonplace book)
FCP	first-class passenger
FRWB	Butcher, Frances Rosamond Wordsworth
FYW	Wordsworth, Frances Young
GCW	Wordsworth, Georgiana Cowan
HBJG	held by Jenny Gibbs (granddaughter of CFW's daughter Toddy)
HBPF	held by Pru Fitzherbert (granddaughter of CFW's daughter Bessie)
TCP	third-class passenger

Acknowledgments

Thank you to everyone who helped me during the writing of this book.

I am particularly indebted to the following members of my family for their generous support, including help with research and other matters: Barbara Feeney, Denis and Cecil Feeney, Geraldine Feeney, Myles Feeney, Pru and Tim FitzHerbert, Jenny Gibbs, Gilbert Haisman, Nic Holdgate, Anna Keedwell, Sandy Knighton, Kamala Patel, Mary Silvester, Larry and Beila Wordsworth.

I also owe a debt of gratitude to the following people for help, advice, inspiration and encouragement of many kinds: Babette Berroth, Julie Biller, Sarah Chisholm, Ian Church, Sandy Rewi Dales, Jette Goldie for the photo of Spylaw House, Lotte Kellaway, Graham Meintjes, Zoë Miller, Tim O'Leary for the photo of the whale's tooth, Di Ponti, Valerie Queva, Lisa Schnapp, Jane Webster, Alouis Woodhouse, Keir Wotherspoon, the staff of the National Library of New Zealand, and the members of the 2008 International Institute of Modern Letters Writers' Group.

I would also like to thank my wonderful editors at HarperCollins, Jo McKay and Amanda O'Connell, and Susan

Morris-Yates, formerly of ABC Books, who originally dreamt up the idea for this book.

This book was written with the assistance of a grant from the International Institute of Modern Letters at Victoria University, Wellington.

Sylvie Haisman was born in New Zealand in 1973, and has spent most of her adult life in and around Sydney, where she went to art school and worked as a technical writer. She recently returned to live in her hometown, Packakariki. Her short fiction has appeared in various Australian and New Zealand publications, and she was a prize-winner in the 2008–09 Commonwealth Short Story Competition. In 2010 she was awarded the Asialink Literature Residency to India. *This Barren Rock* is her first book, and grew out of her 2008 ABC Radio National feature, *Tell Me A Shipwreck*.